IN &
AROUND
THE
CASTLE

By BYRON HANCHETT

Published by Blake Publishing, 2222 Beebee St.,
San Luis Obispo, CA 93401. All rights reserved.
Printed in the United States of America.

ISBN 0-918303-09-5

Dedication

This book is dedicated to Marks Eubanks, my friend and mentor. He knew more about the mechanics of Hearst Castle than any other person. He worked there from 1919 to 1952.

Appreciation

My appreciation is extended to the following persons for their valuable contributions:

Joyce Hanchett - My Wife

Francee Rios - Editor and Typist

Vicki Kastner - Hearst Castle Guide

Bob Latson - Photographer and Hearst Castle Guide

Sherman Eubanks - Marks Eubanks' Son

Allen Russell - Mr Hearst's Pilot

Billie Russell - Mr. Hearst's Airplane Hostess

Harlan Brown - Hearst Ranch Superintendent

Introduction

I would like to take you back to the days when Mr. Hearst was at the Castle, before the State took over. When Mr. Hearst lived there, it was busy with exciting activities and guests. I hope this book will give an insight as to how Mr. Hearst's work reflected what he was really like.

This book is a compilation of some of my memories, which I fervently collected by keeping a diary with dates, stories and events, and taking some of my own pictures. The book has been written in many short stories that are complete in themselves.

Many stories you read here are not given on today's tours of the Castle, nor will you read about them in literature written about the Castle. The only way to know these things was to have been there.

However, this is not a historical book filled with facts and figures, nor does it contain glossy color pictures taken by professional photographers. This is also not meant to be a story about myself, Byron Hanchett. Although I take you through my experiences as "I" remember them, they are meant as reflections of some of those people, events, and things which make up Hearst Castle.

I was hired as an electrician at the Castle under the supervision of Marks Eubanks, back when Mr. Hearst lived at the Castle. Marks worked at the Castle from 1919 to 1952, when he died. I continued to do the maintenance work at the Castle after Marks died, and then spent two years rewiring the Castle after the State took over its operation in 1958. I am retired now, but my experiences working for Mr. Hearst have left a great impression on my life, and I am grateful for this opportunity to share them with others.

Hearst at Play
Left to right – Louella Parsons, W.R. Hearst, Marion Davies.
Sitting – Bill Hearst, Jr.

The Castle

La Cuesta Encantada, or Hearst Castle as it is more commonly known today, is located along the Pacific Coast on Highway 1, halfway between San Francisco and Los Angeles. The Castle is five miles from the Pacific Ocean and stands on a small mountain about 1,600 feet high. The sky serves as a backdrop to silhouette the Castle on top of the mountain.

The Castle is presently surrounded by a 77,000 acre cattle ranch. At one time, this ranch consisted of 275,000 acres, with a 50-mile ocean frontage, including the town of San Simeon near the ocean. There was also a 2,000 acre wild animal compound where herbivorous animals roamed. Parts of the ranch were eventually sold. One part was sold to the government for a military training base, now known as Hunter Liggett.

The Castle is unique. There is nothing in the world with which to compare it. A common misconception is that "Mr. Hearst built the Castle to hold all of his art objects," which sounds like he built a museum to house his art collection —as if the art objects could be removed, leaving behind an empty warehouse. This cannot come close to an appreciation of the true value of the Castle. The Castle itself is one large work of art. It is an excellent example of function and design working together. It is like a giant jigsaw puzzle. Every piece of art serves a purpose, they have a reason for being there. The parts were scattered all over the world at one time, separated by thousands of miles and hundreds of years. The Castle brings together unique features such as large carved wooden ceilings, stone windows, archways, mosaic floors, tapestries, paintings, and even bells. These are an integral part of the Castle. Each object in itself is very unusual — how they harmonize and fit together is truly unique to Hearst Castle.

Hearst tries out his acting skills with Marion Davies.

Features Around The Castle

At one time, the Castle, the ranch, and the town of San Simeon were integrated. It operated much like a city in itself, with many supporting features that helped it to function. The Castle included an airport, a horse ranch, a poultry ranch, dog kennels, orchards with a large variety of fruit, and a cattle ranch with miles of roads and bridle paths.

Many shops were required to build and maintain the Castle, including a carpenter shop, electrical shop, plumbing shop, blacksmith shop, plaster casting shop, and even a large greenhouse for the garden.

The airport, along with a new airplane, served Mr. Hearst and his guests, who were often famous people. For their entertainment, besides the breathtaking view of the Pacific Ocean and access to its beaches, the Castle had two swimming pools, a theatre, tennis court, billiard room, zoo, stables, and a garden with a large variety of flowers. In fact, one person did nothing but take care of the roses.

At one time, the Castle had its own powerhouse. The water

system would serve a small city. The telephone system included a switchboard and a telephone office with a shortwave radio and teletype machine.

If all of these things weren't enough, a visitor could spend months looking at the art and scenery.

My First Day At The Castle

I was hired as an electrician at the Castle on May 3, 1946. I had previously been a projectionist in theatres and had done electrical work for a theatre circuit and in shipyards, but I really wanted experience in electrical construction. My goal was to be an electrician.

During my first day at the Castle, I met Marks Eubanks, the head electrician, in charge of all maintenance. Marks said to me, "The first thing we'll do is take you on a tour of the place." He laughed, saying, "We've got to get rid of that curiosity in your eyes. No one can work when they're looking and wondering about all the interesting things up here."

As we walked, I asked him how long he'd been working at the Castle. He stopped walking and turned to me in answer, "I've been here since 1919. I was here when the Castle was started." Then he looked at me to register my reaction. "I live in San Simeon with my wife, Hazel, and son, Sherman, in the white house on the ocean side near the creek. My wife is the schoolteacher." Marks seemed to apologize for living in one

4

place for so long. After seeing my interest, he continued, "I feel this place is a second home. Some people love it here, and a few — a very few — resent everything here. It's a form of rebellion. You'll understand after you've been here awhile."

I asked Marks what Mr. Hearst was like as an employer. He laughed because there was much to tell. "Well," he said, "if you are trying to do your job, he'll do everything he can to help you. But never tell him that something can't be done, or he might just find someone else who can do it."

"B" House after it was just finished.

He took the handle of the door to the basement of "B" House and said, "In doing my work around here, I try to keep a low profile. I don't work where guests are assembled. If something breaks down, it must be made to work, one way or another, until Mr. Hearst and his guests leave. Then it can be repaired properly. I feel Mr. Hearst has enough on his mind without worrying about some breakdown."

Marks had a good sense of humor, but it was always about his job. He had many things on his mind and much responsibility. We went on under "B" House where he was pulling in a new telephone cable from "C" House. It was hard for me to keep my eyes on the work, and my mind wondered about Mr. Hearst and the environment he had built around himself.

Under "B" House was an interesting place. Hanging on the wall were animal heads of elk and deer, and on the floor were animal heads with unusual horns. Later on I learned these heads were not trophies; they were animals that had died or met with an accident while in the animal compound. Mr. Hearst did not collect animal trophies.

Animal heads hung on the wall under "B" House.

My Fascination With The Castle

When I began work at the Castle I was a country boy and had never seen a life-style such as that at the Castle. The place had much to offer, including Marks Eubanks as a teacher. There were many pieces of equipment to learn, excellent craftsmen with whom to work, famous and unusual guests to observe, and something interesting to see wherever I went. I could not believe that I was going to be paid for this.

The place impressed me so much I started keeping a diary. I kept dates and records of where I worked, as well as stories about the Castle and the people who worked there. Anything that was thrown away became a treasure for my scrapbook. Things that were thrown away then are now collector's items. Anyone who became bored while working there must have had one big callus over all five senses.

In 1946 I started collecting every piece of information I could glean from my experiences at the Castle. In 1949 I wrote an article about the Castle. I asked Marks about different things that happened. I kept that old article, and it has helped me with source facts in writing this new book.

The Activity In 1946 — 47

Much activity was occurring in 1946 and 1947. The old airport hangar was torn down and the new airport and hangar were being built, roads were repaired, and trees were moved. Every house in San Simeon had to be rewired, including all the warehouses. I had the opportunity to wire or rewire every building in San Simeon and on the ranch. I couldn't wait to see inside the beautiful old ranch house.

The poultry ranch was changed into a modern plant. Telephone and power lines were renewed. The new wing was under construction, and guests continued to visit and be entertained. Mr. Hearst seemed to be delighted with all the activity.

Families In San Simeon

In 1947 eighteen families lived in San Simeon, besides the many employees who lived on the hilltop and at the ranch. Briefly giving their names and telling about them will help the reader to understand the town and the operation of the place.

First was Marks Eubanks, my friend and supervisor. He had many responsibilities and the knowledge to cope with them. First he was an electrician. He also knew plumbing, auto mechanics, power and telephone line construction and equipment, and even elevators.

Marks had only one eye. He lost one eye in an accident on the ranch. But he saw more with one eye than most people see with two eyes. I often wondered if I had only one eye, if I would be able to see as much as he did.

I had worked with Marks for two years before I learned he had a degree in electrical engineering, and even then, it was someone else who told me. Marks was the kind of man who if he had an engineering degree in his pocket and a hole in the bottom of his shoe, he would show you the hole in his shoe, and if it helped to do the job, he would have folded up the paper on which the degree was written and put it inside the shoe to cover the hole.

Nigel Keep, the horticulturist, was in charge of designing and planting the gardens. He was hired on January 4, 1922. Norman Rotanzi was his only successor. These two men are the only ones to hold this position. Norman was still there in 1984.

John Harris, the swimming pool man, was the prankster, and sometimes we called him many other things. He usually started some rumor with a whispering campaign.

Frank Frankolich, the stone mason at the Castle, was an artist with rock or marble. He was a very quiet man, even using silence for self-defense.

John Conally took care of the wild animals. He was always ready to share his information about the animals, each of which he knew individually.

John Conally with a zebra in the animal compound.

Bill Reid was the greenhouse man, and Mr. Hughes worked as a gardener at the Castle.

Nick Yost took care of the warehouses and all the antiques. He moved just as fast as he talked. He could move heavy or delicate objects without damaging them. He was also an excellent photographer.

George and Peggy Brunner worked with Nick. Peggy kept the records on the antiques.

Roy Summers was postmaster and bookkeeper.

Leonard Williams was foreman over all farming. His father and brothers also worked for Mr. Hearst in different capacities.

Archie Soto lived in a house on the ranch and was foreman of the cow ranch. He knew all about cattle — he was a real cowboy.

Gene Guthnecht worked at the airport. Al Berger, the chauffeur, did most of the driving for Mr. Hearst.

Lesh Villa was a retired blacksmith who worked on the ranch. He had two sons, Charlie and Harry "Doc". Doc took care of the gate at the entrance to the Castle. Charlie was a cowboy and is still on the ranch. The ranch has always been his home.

Mr. Silacci and Johnny Victorena worked as ranch hands.

Gilbert Petti, a cowboy, lived in a house in San Simeon, but he and his wife often stayed in a cabin at Tobacco, a cow camp twenty miles behind the Castle. Gilbert had a flock of wild turkeys near the cabin, and every time they took him supplies they brought a bag of wheat or corn for the turkeys.

Gilbert's cabin was near a stream of water, and a pipe ran from the stream to the sink in his kitchen. He left the water running in the sink day and night because he liked the sound. One time when I was in his cabin, I got a drink from the sink and then shut off the water. He said to me, "You people come out here, and the first thing you do is shut off my water in the sink." His wife looked at me and smiled, and Gilbert continued, "And to add insult to injury, some of them accuse me of wasting water. Yet they will go outside and stand by that stream watching the water run by and never say anything about waste." He took his hat off, and I could see the scowl on his forehead as he said, "That running water is one of the few luxuries I have." Well, I never turned off his water again. In fact, I drank out of the stream.

One might work at the Castle for more than a year and never know a man's real name; he would be identified by his occupation. These were a few of the people that lived in San Simeon, and many more employees stayed at the ranch in the bunkhouse, at the Castle, and in Cambria.

Ann Miller
Housekeeper To Curator

Ann Miller came to work at the Castle in 1946 on the housekeeping staff. She and I worked together on many different projects over the years. Ann was very aware of the things that went on around her. She was a great help to Marks and I in doing our maintenance work. If anything was broken or did not work right, she knew it.

After Ann was at the Castle a short time, she was promoted to head housekeeper, in charge of planning dinners and hiring waiters and extra help to take care of the guests. She not only worked hard, but also studied the artifacts, their history, and how to best maintain them.

In the late fifties Ann went to work for the State at the Castle and was in charge of the artifacts. Her job was equivalent to a curator. Ann has dusted and handled all the objects in the Castle so many times that if she was blindfolded, she could probably name the object by its feel and indicate where it belongs.

On March 30, 1984, Ann Miller retired. I attended a dinner held in her honor at the Madonna Inn in San Luis Obispo.

Julia Morgan, Architect

Miss Julia Morgan was the architect for the Castle and guest houses. One did not have to know her or her past accomplishments to admire her genius. The design of the Castle was an exacting project.

An architect is usually given a greater building tolerance in other buildings. The rooms are built and then the ceilings are made to fit or the panels on the wall cut to fit. In the Castle, however, the ceilings and walls were considered first, then the rooms were built to fit them.

Miss Morgan's office was a small shack built against the Castle. Blueprints laid on a long table, alongside a small hollow decorated casting that held her pencils. She sat on an old stool, the seat was made of thin plywood. An overstuffed chair was in the office for Mr. Hearst. They worked many hours together in these surroundings.

Before we started wiring the airport, Miss Morgan left the Castle and her office was no longer used. Marks and I took her old blueprint rack to the airport to hold our prints. Then, in

14

1983, Morris Cecil, a guide supervisor, asked me to help him restore Julia Morgan's office as it was back then.

The thin plywood seat of the old stool which Miss Morgan used was very weak, so I started to cut a new piece of plywood to repair it. But Ann Miller said, "No, we keep the same seat and reinforce it. We do not replace anything old with something new."

I had no idea that thirty-seven years later I would be restoring her office for visitors to see. Miss Morgan's office is now shown on one of the tours.

Sherman Eubanks

In the May 1982 issue of *Reader's Digest,* I read a small article about a land developer in California's San Bruno Mountains. This man was trying to develop land and, at the same time, save three endangered species of butterflies. He came up with a habitat conservation plan where he planted lupine and violets on which the butterflies feed. His butterfly surveillance cost him $800,000 in 1982; now it's up to $1.5 million.

I thought what an unusual man. That sounds like something Mr. Hearst would do. I checked back to find his name, and it was Sherman Eubanks, Marks' son. He was also a product of San Simeon.

I had not seen Sherman Eubanks in twenty-four years. I called him and he sent me some notes his mother, Hazel Eubanks, had written in 1974 about her experiences at San Simeon and the Castle.

Hazel taught school in San Simeon and Cambria. She was responsible for putting the college prep course in the Cambria high school in the 1930's, which was then an agriculture school.

Marks Eubanks and his son, Sherman.

Hazel Eubanks' Memories
(In her own words)

The man who knew more about the mechanics of the Castle and worked for the Hearst organization longer than any other man was Marks Eubanks. He was born in 1896 to John and Belle Eubanks in Cambria. He spent his boyhood in Cambria and was familiar with all the country around there and in San Simeon.

Upon his graduation from Cal Poly in San Luis Obispo as an electrical engineer, he enlisted in the Air Force in World War I, and was sent to San Antonio, Texas. After his training there, he was sent to London as an airplane mechanic, where he became an instructor. He then flew to Paris when the Armistice was signed. He was among the first to return, and he immediately went to work at the site of what was to be the Castle.

The first work to be done was to build a fence around the site and construct "shacks" for the workmen. Also, a warehouse had to be built to store and protect the materials and furniture and artifacts as they arrived. Mr. Roy Summers was the caretaker and the first postmaster.

All materials had to be shipped in by boat. The San Antonio brought in supplies regularly to the San

Simeon pier. It whistled when it was ready to dock, and that was the signal for Mr. Eubanks to go down to the pier with a truck and help them unload the boat.

San Simeon was originally a whaling station. Later, it became a village of homes for workers on the Hearst project. Mr. Hearst planned to make San Simeon a modern Spanish village, and he built four beautiful stucco homes for his employees. He planned to tear the old buildings down, but the Depression caused construction to stop in San Simeon as well as at the Castle for the time being.

The first buildings to be built at the hilltop were "A", "B" and "C" Houses, in one of which Mr. Hearst lived until the Castle was ready for occupancy. Before these buildings were ready, he lived with his five sons in the old ranch home at the ranch, the Phoebe Apperson Hearst home.

There was no electricity and lanterns had to be used. So Mr. Hearst had a powerhouse built and a giant dynamotor installed, which Mr. Eubanks operated. One day, the watchman was to turn off the lights at midnight, but he left them on until three A.M., when Mr. Eubanks turned off the main generator and switched to the Pelton water wheel. It so happened that Mr. Hearst was taking a bath at the time, and when the lights went out he became very angry and said to fire the electrician. After the situation was explained to him, Col. Willicombe, Mr. Hearst's top man, informed Mr. Eubanks that everything was okay.

Mr. Hearst was very kind to animals. If anyone drove over fifteen miles per hour through the wild animal compound, they were fired, and if anyone ran into an animal and it was their fault, they were fired.

Mr. Hearst was just as kind to people. In going back and forth from San Luis Obispo in his car, or a taxi driven by Mr. Steve Zegar, he would pick up poor hitchhikers and, upon hearing of their troubles, he would often find jobs for them with his newspapers or in some other capacity.

He took care of all of his employees when they

became ill or needed operations, and he paid all the expenses. When our little girl was severely burned, he offered to send for specialists to try to save her. However, nothing could be done to save her and she died. We appreciated his offer. His resident nurse, Mrs. Katie Marshall, was always ready to help.

After Pacific Gas & Electric (PG&E) ran their power lines to the Castle and San Simeon, Mr. Eubanks took care of the maintenance of these lines. Many nights during a storm, wet and cold, he would go out and work on these high voltage power lines alone. He was also the fire chief and had regular fire drills.

When Mr. Hearst bought two planes, the "Cream Puff" and the "Little Cream Puff," Mr. Eubanks installed border lights and floodlights at the old airport, which is where the Visitor's Center is now.

Many of the guests came by plane. One sad accident happened when the "Little Cream Puff" crashed in the dense fog at the old airport. Lord and Lady Plunkett and the pilot, Tex Phillips, were killed. Mr. Roy Summers, San Simeon's postmaster, was there and, fortunately, escaped injury.

Mr. Allen Russell was the pilot of the big "Cream Puff," and he resided in San Simeon until Mr. Hearst sold the plane before World War II.

The guests also came by train, and Mr. Steve Zegar, with his taxi, met them at the station in San Luis Obispo, along with Mr. Hearst's private cars.

As young boys, Mr. Hearst's sons were very playful and mischievous. When they received Daisy air rifles for Christmas, they didn't bother to go outside to shoot them, but fired into the ceilings of rooms at the ranch house where they were living at the time.

Another time, Mr. Eubanks was replacing light bulbs on top of the Castle, and the boys threw the old bulbs down on the patio to hear and watch them pop. Mr. Eubanks let them have their fun, and then he made them go down and sweep up all the glass.

As the boys grew up, they were very democratic, mingled with the help, and attended public dances in

San Simeon and Cambria. I danced with George Hearst several times.

Mr. Hearst served one cocktail before dinner. He drank only beer. Drinking parties in the guests' rooms were forbidden, and anyone found sneaking liquor into the rooms was ordered from the Castle.

Mr. Hearst enjoyed taking a picnic en route to Jolon, where he and his guests would spend several days at his hacienda there. Emmett Reilly usually went along to do the barbecuing. Mr. and Mrs. Harry Taylor were the managers at the hacienda, and Mrs. Taylor would entertain them with her songs at the piano.

A big party was usually held at the Castle on New Year's Eve and on Miss Davies' birthday. Also, a party was held following the completion of each of her pictures. One party was held for the employees, and a big one for the guests, which often included members of her cast in the picture. They served champagne and brought in a live band for dancing. They even served a musical birthday cake on Miss Davies' birthday. Mr. Eubanks would play the organ that rang the bells at midnight.

Miss Davies also liked to visit the employees' party. She would often dance with some of the employees or members of the band. When she found only beer was being served at the employees' party, she ordered cases of champagne for them.

On hot summer nights, guests would sometimes go down to San Simeon and sleep on the beach. They enjoyed going through the new Spanish-type warehouse, which was built to look like a mission, bell and all. In fact one guest saw an opportunity to make some money. He dressed like a priest and received donations from many tourists.

It was once my pleasure to have "Bunky" Hearst (John Hearst, Jr.) in my school in San Simeon. A car from the hill would bring him down in the morning and pick him up after school. On stormy days and nights, he stayed at my home. He was an "A" student. I was happy to present him his diploma on his graduation from the eighth grade.

After graduation, he attended high school in Cambria for one year. He came to me for help with his homework. Needless to say, three of his classmates decided they needed help too.

Bunky lived alone at the Castle with just the help to watch over him. Bunky was Mr. Hearst's favorite grandson. He would come into Mr. Hearst's quarters, whereas Mr. Hearst's own sons usually had to make an appointment. Mr. Hearst bought Bunky a motorscooter and later a car to go back and forth to school. Bunky is now married and is a professional photographer.

Mr. Rossi was superintendent of construction at the Castle. He was liked by some and hated by others. He decided to separate the electrical work into two categories, construction and maintenance. He named Mr. Eubanks as maintenance electrician, and Mr. Dan Ryan as construction electrician. Mr. Ryan didn't like that, as he knew his job would be over when construction stopped, so he quit.

Mr. Nigel Keep was head gardener. He and Mr. Hearst became good friends, as both loved flowers and trees. He was assisted by Pete Sebastian and August Minoli. The Senate of the California Legislature passed a resolution commending Mr. Keep for his part in beautifying California. He later retired and died at the age of 91 years.

Pete Sebastian left the Castle and took over Sebastian's store, which has since become an historical monument. Mr. Hearst tore the old Sebastian Hotel down and built a new stucco home for the older Mr. and Mrs. Sebastian. All the Sebastian children were born in the old hotel.

Bill Hearst, Jr. went to school in the old San Simeon school house, which is still standing. Miss Mayme Gregory was his teacher. She was one of the people who lived in the old hotel.

Life Magazine was a rival publication, and Mr. Hearst refused to subscribe to it, but he did like to read it. So I would send him my copy every week, which he appreciated. In return, he had a year's worth of issues of Good Housekeeping and Hearst

The old schoolhouse in San Simeon where Bill Hearst, Jr. and Bunky Hearst went to school. Hazel Eubanks was one of the teachers.

Cosmopolitan bound in volumes and instructed Col. Willicombe to send them to me. I later donated them to the County Library.

Miss Davies and her guests liked to work jigsaw puzzles, and she would send them to me when they finished with them.

Marks Eubanks and I were married in 1922. We were blessed with a wonderful son, Marks Sherman Eubanks. He has a lovely wife and three children, now living in San Francisco, California.

Mr. Eubanks worked at the castle from January 1919 until his death in 1952, at the age of 55 years, due to a stroke from hypertension.

I hope my memories haven't bored you.

Hazel Eubanks

The Swimming Pools

The Castle has two large swimming pools; the outdoor Neptune pool, and the indoor Roman pool. We always referred to them as the outdoor and indoor pools.

The Neptune Pool

The Neptune Pool, or outdoor pool, is one of the most expensive privately-owned pools ever built. Besides the statuary, artifacts, and marble in this pool, there are other interesting things. It holds 345,000 gallons of fresh spring water. A 4-inch overflow gutter runs all the way around the rim of the pool at water level. The water overflows evenly all around the pool, showing how level it is after being built all these years. The water running into this overflow then runs under the pool into the filter system, consisting of four large compartments filled with rock, gravel, and sand, and is then pumped back into the pool by a large circulating pump that runs 24 hours a day. Tunnels run under and around part of the pool, making a space to run the pipes and making it easier for maintenance.

This pool is always kept full of water, except for short periods of time to clean and maintain it. The water in the pool maintains at an even temperature as this prevents expansion and contraction, which would cause the pool to crack and leak.

24

The Neptune Pool.

When the pool had to be drained for cleaning and maintenance, a few things had to be considered. First, was there plenty of water in the reservoirs so that refilling it didn't put too large a demand on the water supply? Then, was there plenty of help available to give it a good cleaning? When possible, this was done on a cloudy day so that the sun did not overheat the bottom of the pool. There have always been many methods to clean the pool and the statuary in it. John Harris stood in a boat tied around the base of the statues to clean them, or else he stood on the statues.

North of the outdoor pool down the hill are two large oil burning boilers that heat both pools. The boilers are located near large oak trees that conceal the smoke stacks. Insulated steam pipes run from the boilers to both swimming pools.

On October 12, 1948, they wanted the outdoor pool heated. Marks and I cleaned acorns out of the boiler controls. I had to stay in the boiler room and operate it by hand because one of the oil valves didn't work. This was the last time this pool was heated.

John Harris cleaning the statues in the Neptune Pool. The two live mermaids in the background are actually guests at the Castle.

The two granddaughters of the head housekeeper; taken beside the Neptune Pool in 1946.

South of the outdoor pool under the upper terrace are seventeen dressing rooms. One room had bathing caps, towels, and different sizes of bathing suits for the guests. Four large water heaters heated the water for the showers.

The Castle and grounds, with the Neptune Pool under construction.

The Roman Pool

The Roman pool, or indoor pool, is located under the tennis court and holds 205,000 gallons of water. During fire season this pool was kept full of water, giving another supply of water in case of fire. Now, the State always keeps it full, which is actually better for the pool.

The ceiling of the indoor pool was damaged from leaks in the tennis court floor above. In December of 1949, an engineer, Jim Farney, recommended putting tar on the tennis court floor. This stopped the leak for about three months, but then it started leaking again. The State has since corrected this problem.

There have been many stories about this pool. One story is that salt water from the ocean was pumped into the pool. Some have even called it "the salt water pool". Marks Eubanks told me that someone dumped large amounts of salt in this pool to enable them to float easier. He never would tell me who put the salt in the pool.

The salt did much damage to the floor, the pumps, and the filter system, which were never designed for salt water. The conduits carrying the wires for the alabaster lights around the pool were ruined. We worked for days trying to get the wires out. I still wonder who poured salt in the pool.

28

The Two Towers

The two towers on top of the Castle have many interesting features. Besides design and aesthetics, many of the features are functional. Some of these features include the wind vanes, lightning arrestors, bells, water tanks, and a speaker for music.

In 1926 the two towers were different. They were called cupolas, and they were not built to accommodate bells or even carry their weight. In 1927 the towers were changed to make room for the bells in each tower we see today. In 1928 tile was put on the domes of the towers.

Each tower contains eighteen carillon bells. Each bell has an electric motor, and attached to the motor is a clapper, similar to a small hammer, sitting about two inches away from the bell. Each bell is a different size, giving it a distinct tone. In 1926 the price quoted for the bells was $18,600.

At the entrance to the theatre is an antique organ. The keys on the keyboard are switches that operate the motors on the bells. The organ also had roll records similar to an old player piano. In 1926 the price quoted for the organ keyboard was

The Castle towers when they were called cupolas. A scaffold on the right tower is being used to change the tower to accommodate the bells.

The Castle tower showing the bells, wind vane, and tile dome as it appears today.

$6,850. Before I came to the Castle, Marks would put on a roll recording and play the bells every Christmas.

The bells were made in Tourai, Belgium in 1929. Marcel Michiels was the bell founder. He died in 1931, and so his son came to the Castle in January of 1932 to supervise the installation of the bells. On May 17, 1932, the clappers on the bells had to be changed in order to increase the volume of the sound.

The bells have inscriptions written on them. Bob Latson, a guide at the Castle, and I copied some of these inscriptions:

> *It Cometh into Court and Pleads the Cause of Creatures Dumb   and Unknown to the Laws.*
> *And This Shall Make in Every Christian Clime the Bell of Arti Famous for All Time.*

On another bell is written:

> *Ring in the Christ That is to Be.*
> *Ring in the Valiant Man and Free the Larger Heart the Kindlier Hand.*
> *Ring Out the Darkness of the Land.*

Another inscription:

> *A Thousand Trills and Quivering Sounds, in Airy Circles O'er Us Fly Till Wafted by a Gentle Breeze.*
> *They Faint and Languish by Degrees and at a Distance Die.*

And another:

> *Around, Around, Companions All Take Your Ground, and Name the Bell With You Profound.*
> *Concordia is the Word We've Found.*
> *Tuned be its Metal Mouth Alone to Things Eternal and Sublime.*
> *And as the Swift Wing'd Hours Speed on, May it Record the Flight of Time.*

31

In one of the towers was a speaker shaped like a large horn. The wires from this horn ran to the theatre projection booth and through a switching arrangement. Records could be played on a turntable in the booth, and music came out of the horn in the tower. Announcements could be made by a microphone connected in the booth.

The horn speaker in one of the towers, which was connected to the projection booth sound system.

A speaker in one end of the Refectory was also connected into this system, so the guests could have music during their dinner.

Mr. Hearst owned several radio stations. In cleaning up some of the wiring in the projection booth, I found some of the old wires connected to this system which could also pick up his radio stations.

One time when I ran a movie at the Castle, I found a record of carillon bells that had been recorded in Canada. I played this record, switching the music into the tower horn, with the volume turned up high. The music could be heard in San Simeon and the cowboys could hear it in the back country. Everyone thought it was actually the carillon bells playing. John Harris told all the gardeners that I was the one playing the organ. I was treated with some respect for a few days, until they found out the truth.

Each tower has a wind vane on top, much larger and heavier than they look from the ground.

One day, Mr. Hearst called Marks over to "A" House and he asked Marks, "How is it that when the wind is blowing hard, one wind vane points in one direction, and the other points in a different direction?" Marks told him we would correct it. None of us working there noticed this, but Mr. Hearst did.

Val, the iron worker, and I climbed on top of the tile-domed towers. We found that one wind vane had a hole rusted in it and the bearings were stuck in one place. So we took both wind vanes down, patched, cleaned, painted, greased the bearings, and put them back up. After that when the wind blew, they both pointed in the same direction.

The tiles on the tower domes were cracked and loosened by an earthquake. On November 28, 1952, we climbed on top of the towers with five-gallon buckets and picked up all the loose tile.

We pried off any tiles that were at all loose so they would not fall and hurt someone below. This tile could not be duplicated, so we saved it all. Later, the State repaired the domes, using the old tile we had saved.

When we put in the fire alarm system in 1947 and 1948, the insurance company required that we put in a lightning arrestor (lightning rod) system on top of the towers. A large copper cable is connected to the bearings of the wind vane and goes to the ground where it is grounded.

Elevators
In The Castle

There are two elevators in the Castle. One serves the new wing; the other one we called Mr. Hearst's elevator.

Mr. Hearst's elevator, which was finished and ready for use on October 9, 1928, is just off the assembly room. It was patterned after an old confessional booth. There was never an escape hatch put in the top of this elevator because of the fancy woodwork on the ceiling. Also, some of the elevator equipment sat on top of the ornate wooden ceiling.

In the elevator equipment room was a crank and, in case of power failure, one could crank the elevator up to the next floor. In order to keep this crank accessible, we never locked the door to the equipment room. Every time I oiled or checked this elevator, I made sure the crank was there.

One day I went into the equipment room and the crank was gone. I told Marks, and he pulled the switch on the elevator, shutting it down. I asked him, "Shall I get Val to make another crank?" Marks answered, "No, we'll let the employees walk. When they get tired of walking, they'll put the crank back." At that time Mr. Hearst and his guests were not there.

Any time there were children at the Castle, we locked the equipment room for their safety. About the only children that came to the Castle were Mr. Hearst's grandchildren, Willie and Austin, W. R. Hearst, Jr.'s two boys. The only other child around the Castle was Randy Harris. His parents, Charlie and Hedwig, worked there. Randy is now the head of restoration at the Castle.

The elevator in the new wing has an escape hatch in the ceiling. We always kept a chair in the elevator to stand on to climb through the escape hatch if that ever became necessary. In an emergency, a battery-operated button in the elevator would ring a bell in the kitchen.

I was doing some work at the airport one day, and Marks drove up in a hurry. He said, "Byron, come with me, I need some help." I always liked this kind of duty because it meant something exciting and new was about to happen. As we left the airport, Marks said, "There's a bad relay on Mr. Hearst's elevator. It will not pull in." I asked him, "Why don't you shut it down until you get another relay?" Marks responded, "There are some people at the Castle to study the Grecian pottery up in the library and they need the elevator."

I was always amazed at how Marks could work his way out of these kinds of situations. I asked him, "Where are you going to get a new relay?" He laughed and said, "I just picked up a relay. It's you. You're not new, but you'll do," and he laughed again. Well, I soon found out what he meant. I stayed in the elevator equipment room all day. When anyone pushed the button to use the elevator, the relay would hum. Then I would push the relay with my finger. At lunch time, Marks brought me pheasant, all cut up, and two pieces of apple pie. With a grin, he said, "You can eat with one hand, like an Arab, and keep your relay hand out of the food." In spite of such good service, it was a long day.

The Assembly Room

The Assembly Room is the largest room in the Castle. It is eighty-three feet long, thirty-one feet wide, and the ceiling is twenty-four feet high. There are sixty light fixtures, with five sixty-watt lamps to each fixture, making a total of 300 light bulbs. The fixtures weigh about fifteen pounds each and are fastened to the ceiling with steel wire.

One night when I came to the Castle to run a movie, Ann Miller was playing the piano in the north end of the Assembly Room. She was playing "Around the World in Eighty Days," when I glanced up at the ceiling to check the lights, and right over her head I noticed a fixture that had broken loose. It was hanging by only the electric wires. I held up my hands to stop her. She asked, "Is my playing that bad?" I pointed up to the light fixture and said, "No, the playing is okay, but that light fixture isn't." We immediately roped off the area to make it safe.

The next day, we had the job repairing this fixture. Marks and I had to find a way to get above the ceiling. We decided there should be a loose panel somewhere, which we found near the broken fixture. I removed the panel and stuck my head above the ceiling with a flashlight. To my surprise, the space above this ceiling looked like a forest of white birch trees. This ceiling is suspended, hung with sisal, a hemp hair-like fiber used to make rope and cord.

The sisal was as big around as my arm. It had been dipped and soaked in white plaster and draped over large steel beams, with each end of the sisal plastered right into the ceiling. The ceiling hangs about thirty inches below the steel beams. The plaster keeps the sisal from deteriorating. Rodents will not chew on it, and it adds strength by becoming part of the ceiling.

No one had crawled above this ceiling since it was built. It would not bear a person's weight and no provisions were made to get above it. So we built a hanging scaffold which hung from the steel beams and ran the length of the ceiling. After Ann's experience, we decided to take a look at all the other fixtures. We repaired two more fixtures, and then left the scaffold for others to use.

We used an extension ladder to relamp this room. The top of the ladder rested on a narrow beam, which we climbed very carefully so that it would not shake. John Harris helped me relamp this room. I liked working with John because he never tried short cuts or came up with any wild ideas.

The New Helper

I always kept an eye on new employees because of the expensive and fragile things in our work environment. New employees always had new ideas, most of which had already been tried.

A new helper was hired to help me. The first day, he worked with me relamping the assembly room. I explained to him that we didn't move anything in the room, that we worked the ladder around the furnishings. The first thing he did was grab hold of a round marble top mosaic table to move it out of our way. The marble top weighed about 100 pounds, and it slid off its wrought iron frame and onto the floor, just missing his foot, and broke into hundreds of pieces. When Marks told Mr. Hearst of the accident, all he said was to call the warehouse in San Simeon and tell Nick Yost to bring up another table. So Mr. Yost brought another table and picked up the pieces of the broken one. He later put the broken one back together, and it was like new.

In the shop we had a light bulb changer, which consisted of

rubber-covered springs to grip the bulb and a handle twenty feet long. One day, the new helper took this into the assembly room. He broke one light bulb and twisted another off in the socket. So, out came the extension ladder.

His next short cut was to lean the ladder against a large tapestry hanging on the wall. Ann caught him at this caper, and this was the last time he helped in the assembly room. After that, if anyone helped me in the assembly room, I told

The Refectory with banners and silver on display.

them, "If you have any new ideas, we'll discuss them after we relamp."

I then took the new helper into the Refectory, where we were relamping the lights on the wall between the Sienese banners. He climbed up between the flags with a screwdriver in his back pocket and tore a hole in one of the flags. The banners were so old they were brittle.

I continued to call this man "the new helper" because I knew he was not going to be around long enough to be called "old". He was like a burro in a penthouse.

The final straw came when he and I were working in "B" House. Ann was there and, for his benefit, she politely indicated, "Please do not eat or bring any food into "B" House." After lunch when I did not see him, I went back to "B" House. There he was, laying spread-eagle on his back, right in the middle of Cardinal Richelieu's bed — shoes and all! I yelled at him to get off the bed, to which he responded in an unconcerned manner, "I wasn't eatin' nothin'." That was his last day. We gave him his "hay" and sent him down the hill.

The Theatre

Before the theatre was built, in May of 1924, Mr. Hearst had movies run for the construction workers once a week. He would pay someone $30 to run a seven-reel show that lasted about one hour. The projectionist furnished the film and used portable picture machines.

The theatre seats fifty people, and Mr. Hearst always sat in the front row. The seats were set back from the screen to make better viewing. A telephone sat on a small table near Mr. Hearst's chair. This phone was connected through the telephone office, and he could talk to the projectionist in the booth, telling him to start the show or to raise or lower the sound. In a standard theatre, they used a buzzer. One buzz meant to raise the sound, two to lower it, and three meant there was trouble with the picture.

Mr. Hearst had good theatre equipment and the sound was excellent. The crimson silk brocade on the walls served two purposes. Besides being decorative, it also improved the sound acoustics, along with the large soft chairs and plush carpet.

Another feature in the theatre is the caryatids on both walls, made and installed in August of 1930. These large ornate ladies not only held the house lights, but their large figures helped break up the sound on the long straight walls. In a standard theatre, the bigger the audience the better the sound. In this theatre, the sound was good even if it was empty.

A view inside the theatre.

The large screen on the stage had a motor with cables connected to it. The screen could be lowered into the basement to clear the stage for a stage show or for cleaning.

Outside the theatre, near the projection booth, the State cut a doorway for visitors to exit from the theatre. Right where this exit was cut, there used to be a large metal film locker.

I remember one film in which Miss Davies starred, entitled "Page Miss Glory".

In those days, film was very flammable and very dangerous, giving off a toxic gas if it caught fire. Projection booths were often lined with metal. The wall between the booth and the audience had metal shutters that slid down

Miss Davies starred in "Page Miss Glory"; picture taken in 1935.

automatically to close the audience off in case of fire.

Under the projection booth is a very large 2,300 volt generator, which changed the electrical current from alternating to direct current. With this very large generator and high voltage, many thought this was an unwise and unnecessary expenditure on Mr. Hearst's part, but not so. In the 1930's and early 1940's, the voltage fluctuated badly, and this large generator acted like a flywheel, giving an even light on the screen. This generator is so large, it has never been moved and is still in its original location today.

"Gone With the Wind", released in 1939, was shown in this theatre before it was ever premiered. This picture had four miles of film and ran four hours, starring Clark Gable and Vivian Leigh.

After Mr. Hearst left the Castle, his sons occasionally came to the Castle and used the theatre. On one occasion when they wanted a show, I went up early to check the equipment, since it hadn't been used for some time. Pack rats had carried acorns into the machines, so I took them apart, cleaned and oiled them, and repaired a speaker cable, and then everything worked fine.

Many times, two shows were run, an early show for the employees, and a late show for the guests.

One night while I was running a show, right in the middle of the show someone was on stage waving their arms. I turned the house lights on and the sound off. I raised the glass between the audience and the booth. It was David Hearst. He called to me, "Do you have any more film up there?" I answered, "Yes, I have three more pictures." He said, "Please start another show. We can't stand this one." So I picked out a picture I liked, entitled "High Noon", starring Gary Cooper and Grace Kelly, and ran another show. I have run many shows in my career, and many times I would have liked to have stopped one picture and started another. This was the first time I actually got to do so — and I loved it.

When I ran shows at the Castle, I was allowed to bring two guests with me. Sometimes I brought my wife, Joyce, or my children. One time I took two little girls, my daughter Judy, and her friend, Tony Williams, who has since married, and her name is Tony Evans. She is now a guide at the Castle. Once, I took my oldest son, Byron Lindsey Hanchett. Emmett Reilly was cooking at the time. He took my son to the refrigerator and gave him a large turkey leg. I was ready to start the show, and here's this kid with a huge turkey leg almost as big as he was. This was a very funny sight and Emmett followed him around laughing. I told my son he would have to put the leg back or he couldn't see the show. So he gave it back to Emmett, who saved it for him for later.

Sometimes I brought adult guests with me, and I always gave them a little tour before the show. They would look at a statue or painting and would have to know who made it, how old it was, or how much it cost before they knew if they liked it.

On December 7, 1965, I was working for the State rewiring the Castle. They had me disconnect all the equipment in the projection booth. I thought December 7 was a good date to pull the plug on the theatre.

A. E. Barnhizer and Byron Hanchett changing the electricity to the theatre in 1965 while rewiring the Castle for the State.

46

This was the final step in changing from one era into another. Sometimes progress is sad. It reminded me of condemning a home to build a much-needed freeway. I ran the last movie in this theatre, "The Brave Warrior," a fitting title for the last show.

The Dentist Room

Above the projection booth was a small room that was converted into a dentist office. Dr. Luiz Pereira of San Luis Obispo was the dentist. He told Mr. Hearst what equipment he needed. The dentist chair had an air compressor connected to it, and hot and cold running water, a sink, and extra electrical outlets were installed.

Dr. Pereira was also my dentist, so I knew him well. He told me Mr. Hearst was a good patient, but that he had to know about everything that was happening. Dr. Pereira said, "I gave Mr. Hearst a running commentary on everything I was doing and explained what I was going to do before I did it. He was a very inquisitive man."

Mr. Murphy, the barber in Cambria, would come up the hill and trim Mr. Hearst's hair while he sat in the same dentist chair. Mr. Murphy was also my barber for a number of years. He related his story to me, "Mr. Hearst only wanted his hair trimmed. I never used the word 'cut' around him. If I did, he would correct me. The word was 'trim'." Mr. Hearst had a

47

saying, "If you can see a haircut, then it's not very good."

Many of the maids, telephone operators, and other women who worked at the Castle used the dentist room to wash and fix their hair. They kept their shampoo in a cupboard with their names written on the bottles.

Bunky, Mr. Hearst's grandson, did not like the fact that the maid who cleaned his room was always going through everything he kept in his room. He told her not to do this, but she continued. So one night, Bunky went to the dentist room and poured all the shampoo out of her bottle and filled it with pancake syrup. That put a stop to her snooping.

In the early 1950's, we disconnected and removed the dentist chair and air compressor. I didn't like doing this because I could no longer say, "This place even has its own dentist chair." It seems like every change reduced the place a little more.

The
Layout Room

A large room under the theatre, the same size as the theatre, was to have been the bowling alley, but it was used as a layout room. This was where most of the giant jigsaw puzzles (the parts and pieces of the castle) were put together. Large stone windows were laid out on the floor. The pieces were assembled, numbered, and the overall dimensions written on strips of thin plywood laid on the floor beside them. Then they were ready to be placed in reinforced concrete openings.

Archways were on the floor, the pieces numbered and the key stone at the top ready to lock in all the other pieces. My favorite archway is the one overhead between the breakfast room and the Refectory. This archway has thirteen stones. Most archways have an uneven number of stones.

On one side of the layout room, long rows of light fixtures hung from the ceiling. Some of these fixtures were so old they were made for candles, and many of them had not been wired for electricity. Some lantern-type fixtures had as many as twenty windows, and I had to look close to see how to get into

Back of Castle — reinforced concrete waiting for the windows to be installed.

them. The small windows were sealed together with lead and sometimes silver.

Marble and alabaster lamp standards lay scrambled on the floor. The conduit to thread down the center to hold the pieces together had not yet been cut.

Knowing some of these craftsmen and watching them put things in place was a very interesting experience for me. I am more interested in seeing a sculptor make a statue or a painter paint a picture than to see the finished product. A sculptor once said, "You do not chip a face out of marble. You chip out everything that is not the face."

The Fur Vault

In the theatre basement, near the layout room, are the antique vaults. One of these vaults was made into a fur vault in September of 1946 by the Herman Safe Company.

Refrigeration was installed in the vault. However, there was never any equipment installed to control the humidity. This made a bad situation, as we had to check the vault often to make sure the furs were okay.

All kinds, shapes, colors, and sizes of furs were in this vault, including men's sheepskin coats, which looked out of place hanging alongside the beautiful furs.

Green Fur Coats

One time Marks and I went into the back country to work on the telephone lines and left one of the men in our department in charge of checking the fur vault. A few weeks later when we returned, I went to check the furs. The moment I opened the door my nose told me something was wrong. I turned on the light, and all those beautiful fur coats had turned green with mold an inch long. Someone had accidentally dropped a rag on the refrigerator motor belt, stalling it and blowing a fuse.

I went back to the electric shop and told Marks. After we got over our panic, we took all the coats and put them in cardboard boxes. We made three trips carrying them to the roof of the Castle. We spread them out on the tile roof in the sun to dry. While they dried, I brushed them with a stiff brush and Marks cleaned, sprayed, and got the fur vault back in operation. I brushed those coats all day, and after the coats were hung back in the vault, it took three five-gallon buckets of water to wash the green mold off the red tile roof.

No one ever found out about this. Marks and I never said

anything to anyone, not even to the man who should have been checking the fur vault. Then, about two years later, on June 3, 1949, Ann Miller and I carried the coats out of the vault to air them. Ann cleaned and sprayed the vault, and I tightened the belts and oiled the refrigerator motor. I asked Ann, "How do the coats look?" She said, "They look all right, but they don't smell so good."

The Kitchen
And The Cooks

The cook at the Castle was Dally Carpio. Some called him Dally, and others called him Dolly, but everyone was careful what they called him. His movements were quick and he was an artist at cutting up vegetables with his large knife. No one fooled with Dally. I don't know if it was because of the large knife, or his rapport with Mr. Hearst.

When Dally left the Castle, Emmett Reilly took over as cook. Emmet worked on the ranch and at the Castle from 1934 until 1973, and he lived either at the ranch or the Castle all that time. Emmett was the epitome of freedom. He would come and go as he pleased. The reason management probably put up with this was because of the many things he could do.

Emmett could cook barbecue over an open fire on round up, he could build a fence, or dress a lamb chop. He loved the large stove in the kitchen and he knew how to operate it.

Emmett was a funny man with a great sense of humor. When he told a story, you knew he had been there when it happened. He would tell the story with a twist that would put

MENU

La Cuesta Encantada   San Simeon, California

October 11, 1946

Luncheon

SALAD

SCRAMBLED EGGS WITH SLICED HAM

CODFISH CAKES CREAM SAUCE

HASHED BROWNED POTATOES

BOILED SMALL ONIONS

FRUIT   ICE   COOKIES

DINNER

FRIED SCALLOPS TARTER SAUCE

BROILED GUMBO SQUABS MUSHROOMS

JULIENNE FRIED POTATOES

BUTTERED GREEN PEAS

CHERRY PIE   ICE   COOKIES

"STALLION ROAD," WITH ZACHARY SCOTT AND
ALEXIS SMITH. FROM WARNER BROS. STUDIOS.
SHORT FROM WARNER BROS. STUDIOS.

Breakfast 9:00 to 12:00   Luncheon 2:00   Dinner 9:00

Menu. October 11, 1946

54

GUEST LIST

"A" HOUSE

L. F.	R. F.
L. B.	R. B.
HERO	SHIELD

"B" HOUSE

L. F. Mr. Hanes	R. F. Mr. Gortatowsky
L. B. Mr. Baskervill	R. B. Mr. Howey

"C" HOUSE

L. F. Mr. W.R. Hearst, Jr.	R. F. Mr. & Mrs. Geo. Hearst
L. B. Mr. John Hearst	R. B. Mr. David Hearst
L. TOWER Bunky	R. TOWER
L. TERR.	R. TERR.

CLOISTERS

No. 1 Mr. Mitchell	No. 3 Mr. Howard
No. 1 Mr. Walker	No. 3 Mr. Becker
No. 2 Mr. Lindeman	No. 4
No. 2 Mr. Anderman	No. 4

CASTLE

S. DECK	N. DECK
S. DUP. U.	N. DUP. U.
S. DUP. L.	N. DUP. L.
S. CEL. Mr. Lindner	N. CEL. Mr. Shea
S. DOGES	N. DOGES

1st Floor Over Billiard Room	GOTHIC -- Mr. MacKay
2nd Floor Over Billiard Room	Mr. Carrington
3rd Floor Over Billiard Room	

Guest list. May 24, 1947

The large kitchen stove run by a water wheel.

O'Henry to shame.

Sometimes Emmett would have a lost weekend, and sometimes the weekend ran into weeks. Many times, if guests were coming to the Castle, Ann would send someone to town to find Emmett. They would try to get him up the hill at least two days early.

In the mornings at the Castle, we all lined up in front of the counter near the large stove. This is where we gave Emmett our breakfast orders.

One morning we were giving our orders, and it came Ross Hamilton's turn. Ross was a friendly, methodical man who worked in the garden, and he loved to visit and talk. Emmett always had to ask Ross for his order and, then again, Emmett would have to ask him how he wanted it cooked. Ross offered nothing, everything had to be pried out of him with another question. This particular morning, Emmett did not feel so good. Emmett asked, "Ross, what will you have?" Ross answered, "Bacon, eggs, and a large stack of hot cakes," and continued talking. Emmett never asked him another thing. He fried his bacon, cooked his hot cakes, and put them on his plate. Then Emmett took two whole raw eggs, without cracking the shells, and put them in the skillet, whipped butter over the shells, and laid them on Ross' plate near the bacon and hot cakes. Ross was still talking. He was in the dining room before he noticed the eggs. He came back and said to Emmett, "Emmett, I didn't want boiled eggs." Everyone was laughing, and Emmett answered him, "Ross, those eggs are not boiled. They are just exactly the way your ordered them — not up, not over, just eggs. I even gave you butter on them for good measure." After that, Ross always turned in his order giving all the details.

All the equipment in the kitchen was either large or unusual in design, such as the kitchen stove, which is still there. It is about ten feet long, with warming ovens and coils to heat hot water. The thick iron plates varied in temperature according to their distance from the burner. The cook would pick the plate on the stove for the temperature he wanted. The burner has two impellers, one on the bottom and one on the top. A small jet of water, controlled by a valve, hits the impeller on the bottom, causing it to turn. The oil then hits the impeller on the top, atomizing the oil, and throwing it back into the burner. This is the only stove I have ever seen that is run by a water wheel. Who ever heard of turning up the water on a stove to make it hotter?

There was also an electric toaster about eighteen inches square, a large food mixer near one wall, and even an ice cream freezer with an electric motor.

The old battery-operated clock that hung over the counter near the stove is still there. It was always slow; it was only right twice in twenty-four hours and when we set it. The only time anyone looked at it was when they needed an excuse for being late.

There were large walk-in refrigerators under the dining room where all the meat was aged, and four large refrigerators in the kitchen area; two for the kitchen, one for the guests, and the other one for the help. We never got into the kitchen or guest refrigerators. The help's always had more in it anyway. It had all the food left over from the kitchen and the guests. There was cold chicken, pheasant, duck, steak, pie, cake, and all kinds of other goodies.

John Harris and I worked together on many jobs. Besides eating breakfast and lunch at the Castle, we would raid the kitchen at 10 a.m. and again at 2 p.m. We never cut a pie, we took the whole pie, and a half of chicken each, or whatever was there. We'd usually go under the outdoor pool to have our little snacks. After about two years of this, we gained so much weight we had to tie each other's shoes.

When Mr. Hearst left the Castle in 1947, there were a lot of us who lost some weight. It's no wonder that very few people ever quit a job at the Castle.

The Beer Sign

Tommy Tomblin, the painter, came to the electric shop and told us he was going to paint the kitchen and pantry area, and he wanted us to move out all the portable appliances and build a scaffold for him.

While doing this job, I noticed a small sign typed in capital letters on a piece of yellow paper, hung on the wall with four thumb tacks. It read: "By instructions of Mr. Hearst, no hard liquor is to be served to anyone after dinner. Beer is okay." This sign sheds light on Mr. Hearst's liquor policy and should quelch any rumors of wild parties held at the Castle.

This little sign hung in the butler's pantry for years. When we took it off the wall to throw away, I kept it — more scrapbook material.

```
BY INSTRUCTIONS OF MR. HEARST NO

HARD LIQUOR IS TO BE SERVED TO ANYONE

AFTER DINNER.

    BEER IS O.K.
```

The beer sign in the butler's pantry.

Wine Labels

Ann Miller called the electric shop one day and asked me to meet her in the wine cellar because some of the lights were burned out and one was broken off in the socket. I took a flashlight and some light bulbs to the cellar, and I picked up a small wooden box in the wine cellar to catch the broken glass and old light bulbs.

When I got back to the electric shop, I threw the box and glass into the trash can. The box landed bottom side up, and on the bottom of the box were some beautiful shipping labels. Two of them were railway express labels, and the other one was an address label done in yellow, black, and red, with a black border. It was addressed to "Mr. W. R. Hearst, San Simeon, California". I saved the bottom of this box and framed it.

Years later, I discovered that some people collect these shipping labels as a form of art. Mike, my youngest son, now has it hanging in his house in Cambria.

Norman Rotanzi
And The Gardens

As much planning went into the Castle grounds as inside the Castle itself. The landscape was planned around the buildings and the existing trees.

It would be difficult to write about the landscape without telling about Norman Rotanzi. Norman came to work at the Castle in 1934. He worked at many jobs until he went to work for Nigel Keep on the grounds, and he has been in that department ever since. The Castle was his home, he lived there at one time. He has been in charge of the grounds for forty years and is still head groundsman.

On November 18, 1982, Norman received an Outstanding Achievement Award from the Groundskeeping Management Society of Pikesville, Maryland. He is only the eighth person in eighty-one years to be honored, and the only one from California.

On March 26, 1984, I attended a party at the Castle in his honor celebrating his fiftieth anniversary of work at the Castle.

Before the State took over the Castle, Norman and his men were responsible for a much larger area. The large fruit orchard had to be pruned, and an orange grove and the pergola had to be watered and tended.

Entrance to the pergola.

The pergola is a large arbor trellis, consisting of parallel colonnades supporting an open roof of girders. Large wires were stretched along the sides of the pergola, and fruit trees and grape vines were trained espalier style on these wires.

Tree with limbs on wires espalier style on the sides of the pergola.

Construction began on the pergola in 1931, which was close to a mile long. It was like driving through a beautiful tunnel. Many mornings, my helper and I would drive through the pergola on our way to work and pick fruit to eat on the job.

Road to the Castle showing the relationship of the pergola to the Castle.

John Bullard
And His Roses

John Bullard did nothing else but take care of the roses. He often grafted several varieties on one rose bush. Sometimes he would tell me about the vitamin content in rose hips, while chewing a rose hip on one side of his mouth. His teeth were missing on the other side, but that seemed to enhance the smile he always had.

John also told me how to make a tabletop of rose petals. He gathered sacks of rose petals, and crushed the petals into an emulsion, spreading them on an old table. When they dried, one could work them like wood, giving a texture to the top. I never tried it, but I loved to hear John talk about roses.

John Bullard, the rose man.

The Birds
And The Bees

Every year the swallows would come and build their mud nests under the eaves of the Castle. After the eggs hatched and the birds left their nests, the old nests would be left plastered all over the fancy wooden eaves. We would drive the fire truck into the yard of the Castle and wash the old nests down with the fire hose. This became sort of an official fire drill.

On the north side of the Refectory, outside under the eaves, was a bee hive. You could see the golden honey in this hive, which was about seven feet long, three feet wide, and two feet thick. The Castle grounds were like bee heaven for the bees with all the flowers. This hive was there for a number of years and we watched it grow, but it eventually had to be removed so maintenance could be done on the woodwork.

The New Wing

When the new wing, the last phase, was under construction, two classes of employees worked at the hilltop. They were the Stolte construction workers and the Hearst employees. Many of the Stolte workers ate and slept at the construction camp set up near the Castle. All of the Hearst employees ate at the Castle or the bunkhouse at the ranch.

One Stolte craftsman that worked on the new wing was Johnny McFadden. He was an excellent mechanic; he could do cement work, lay any kind of floor, and was a good electrician. McFadden laid all the red tile floors in the new wing. He did a perfect job on these floors. The first time Mr. Hearst walked into the new wing, the first thing he did was look at all the floors and said, "Couldn't the man have at least made just one little mistake?" The floors look like they had been laid by a machine. Every time I walk into the new wing, I always look at the floors first. I think McFadden even upstaged some of the old artists.

One day as I was putting the telephone system in the new

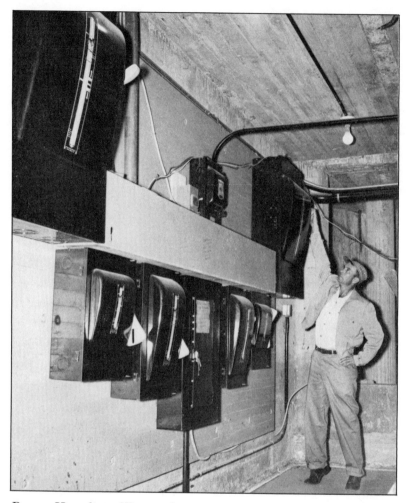

Byron Hanchett. We put these switches up when the new wing was built in 1947.

wing, there was an artist working on the archways in the rooms. This artist was a Frenchman who wore a French beret. He was painting a scene on one of the archways. It looked like a fairytale. I asked the Frenchman, "What does this painting represent?" He answered, "This painting tells a story." In an effort to glean more information, I asked, "What is the story about?" He turned toward me, looked down from the ladder, and said, "Hell, I don't know what the story is about! Make up your own story, or would you have me get down off this ladder and hold you on my knee while I tell you a story." Then he stopped painting, put his brush on the palette and laughed, seemingly pleased with his clever little sarcastic speech. I would like to have curled his beret with one of my speeches, but I didn't. He knew I would take sarcasm for information — but he had no story or information; all he had was a smart tongue.

I told this story to Vicki Kastner, one of the lady guides at the Castle, and she informed me that this artist had to be Camille Salon, quite a famous artist. It's probably better that I didn't know that at the time.

Camille Salon also worked on the ceiling of the Roman Pool in 1932. He had his own ideas about the designs and wanted to change them. He held up the work for awhile and was quite a problem, but a good artist nevertheless.

Frank Frankolich
Stone Mason

The stone mason who worked on the new wing was Frank Frankolich. On March 24, 1948, Frank was finishing some steps in the new wing.

Frank was an older man. He talked like a machine gun, in explosions. He was from the old country and spoke with broken English. When you looked into his eyes you could see little white scars all over his eyeballs. He explained to me that these scars were caused by little chips of stone and marble hitting him in the eyes — and there he was, still chipping with no glasses or goggles. I asked him, "Frank, why don't you wear goggles?" He said, "I don't need them. Every time I chip, I blink my eyes." I asked him, "Well then, why are your eyeballs all scarred up?" He laughed and said, "I got those while I was learning to blink."

I looked down at his tools. They were in an old, open, wooden carpenter box. He had a level with only one smooth edge. The bubble in the glass could only be seen from one side. The other side was encrusted with dried mortar. He had a hammer with a very short handle. It was not a claw hammer, not a ball-peen hammer, and it surely wasn't a stone hammer. I picked up his hammer. The end of the short handle was all battered over where he had tapped marble to level it. That was why the handle was short, he had worn it out. I thought, this hammer looks like Frank; it's short and scarred and has a lot of character. Frank caught me examining his hammer. As he took it from me I commented, "Some hammer." He explained, "That's not a hammer! That's a beatin' iron!" His small cement trowel, once sharp on the end, was worn round and blunt. He had an old stiff brush with part of the bristles missing. In the bottom of the box were some small wooden wedges. He had used these many times to level marble. The wedges were all water soaked and splintered. He even saved some of the splinters off the wedges.

As a rule, Frank was not very talkative. He had a very subtle sense of humor, however, he loved attention. The only way I could get him to talk and enjoy his humor was to pester him. I asked him, "Why don't you get rid of this junk and get yourself some new tools?" That brought him up off his knees. It was as if I had insulted his mother. In total disgust, he said to me, "You just don't understand. These tools fit my hands." He pointed to his shoes, stained and spotted with cement, and he continued, "These tools are comfortable like this old pair of shoes." Then he threw a couple cliche's at me, "An artist needs no brush. A mechanic needs no tools." I said to him, "You sure have proved that last statement," and I left. As I rounded the corner I could hear him laugh.

I have learned one special thing from many of the older men that worked at the Castle. That is, if a young man is not too impatient and takes the time to listen to some of these older men, he can learn many things. The older the man, the more patience it takes to gain information from him, because he has learned to never be hurried.

Frank left the Castle on June 20, 1948. He left his tools and the old tool box in the basement under the theatre. He was going home to the old country to retire and had no further use for the tools. Every time I walked by his tool box, I looked at the hammer and I could hear him say, "They fit my hands." I sure would love to have had that hammer.

New Wing Finished

On April 8, 1948, George Massey, a plumber who worked for Mr. Rankin, the plumbing contractor, came back to the Castle to add some final work on the new wing. I had just finished adding the electrical system to the steam heat in the theatre and was hanging the last light fixture on the new wing stairway. George came over to tell me good-bye. We talked about this being the day the new wing was completed.

Cleaning
The Two Fountains

The two tall circulating fountains below "A" and "C" Houses were plugged up with dirt and leaves, and I was instructed to put them back in operation.

The fountain below "A" House.

The fountain below "A" house has a statue of a small lady on top, with a small basin on the top and a large catch basin on the bottom. When I leaned the ladder against the small top basin, the large lower basin held the ladder out so far that it was in a very precarious position. So I held the ladder and let my six-year-old son, Mike, climb into the small top basin and clean it out.

On top of the fountain below "C" House is Donatello's David with his foot on Goliath's severed head. When I put Mike in the top of this basin, he was just about the same size as David. With Mike's help, we got the water spilling over the fountains again.

The fountain below "C" House as it looked when it was first installed. Notice the design of the tile on the bottom basin.

The tile on the bottom basin of the fountain below "C" House has since been changed. Notice there are no lights or banisters around the stairway. The lower left of the picture shows where electrical wires have been pulled for the lights.

The fountain below "C" House as it appears today. The lights and banisters have been added around the stairway.

Mark Pattersen
Night Watchman

One cold winter night when the mud puddles had turned to ice and the wind was blowing broken branches across the sidewalks, Mark Pattersen, the night watchman, was making his rounds. Mark was an older man, and he was wearing a little short jacket. Mr. Hearst was staying in "A" House, when he saw Mark that night. Mr. Hearst called Mark inside and said to him, "Mr. Pattersen, I want you to go to the housekeeper and get the key to the fur vault. Pick yourself out one of those long sheepskin coats. Get one you like and one that fits. Any time the weather is like this, I want you to wear that coat." Mark picked out his coat and was very proud of it. I think the fact that Mr. Hearst gave him the coat kept him warmer than the coat itself.

The
Gatehouse And Gates

We started wiring the gatehouse on August 13, 1947. Someone was stationed at the gatehouse twenty-four hours a day. Doc Villa had this job; he even slept there. Every employee was issued a pass, which indicated the employee's name and occupation. If Doc happened to get upset with someone, he would make them show their pass before opening the gate, even if he had known them for twenty years.

HEARST ESTATE

GATEMAN: Date _June 19, 1946_

Please admit the bearer,

Byron Hanchett

                      Bearer's Signature

Gate pass issued in 1948.

Trip gate, so guests could open and close the gate without leaving the safety of their cars.

80

We mounted two 1,000 watt flood lights from the old airport on a high metal pipe at the gatehouse. One light shined on the cars coming up the hill, and another light shined on the cars going down the hill.

The gates at the gatehouse each had a long wooden arm with a rope attached to the end. The gate was opened or closed by pulling down on the rope, which moved the long wooden arm attached to a mechanism on the gate.

Other gates farther up the hill operated by a long piece of pipe connected to an eccentric. Cars ran over one pipe to open the gate, and another pipe on the other side to close it. The purpose for these gates was to keep the wild animals in the compound and the visitors in their cars.

My car going through the trip gate.

The Old Airport

On May 10, 1946, we tore down the hangar at the old airport, which is now the site of the present visitor's center. We salvaged all the wire and light fixtures, which were then used on the ranch. Runway lights stood four feet high and ran around the perimeter of the airfield.

A telephone line ran from the airport to the Castle, and fastened to these same telephone poles was a pair of electric wires. These wires ran from the airport to a remote control switch in the telephone office. This made it possible for the telephone operator to turn on the airport lights from the Castle.

Anyone flying to the Castle would call ahead, and upon arriving, they would fly over the Castle and buzz it with the plane, giving the telephone operator the signal to turn on the lights and send a car for them.

The day before we tore the old hangar down, George Hearst, Mr. Hearst's oldest son, flew to the Castle. He had not called ahead. It was during daylight hours and he buzzed the Castle and landed at the airport. No car came for him. He went to the hangar to phone the Castle, but the phone was locked inside and he couldn't get to it. This caused him much inconvenience. He immediately wrote a letter stating that a telephone should be put outside the new hangar. The next day, as the old hangar was being torn down, a construction worker heard about George Hearst's experience and pointed to the old wrecked hangar and said, "That's what happens when you lock the phone away from George Hearst."

The first airport. The runway is L-shaped, with the hangar in the corner of the "L" in the center of the picture. The old pier is in the lower left corner. Two roads, one to the Castle and the other from the Castle, are at the top center of the picture. Old Highway 1 runs across the bottom of the picture.

The New Airport

On September 23, 1946, we started wiring the new airport. We wired the control tower on top of the hangar for radio control, and connected an intercommunication system inside

The new airport hangar in 1947 and the road leading to it.

the hangar. The new runway is eight-tenths of a mile long with 48 surface lights. These lights have a thick glass in a heavy frame set in a concrete base. They were made to support the weight of a plane.

A kitchen was installed in the new hangar with an electric stove to prepare food to take on the plane. In 1983 I found this old stove with the same cord and plug I had put on it in 1946. This stove has made the rounds. It came from the old ranch house, to the airport, and then to the Castle kitchen for Ann Miller to use. She is now the curator at the Castle.

Allen Russell went to work for Mr. Hearst as his pilot in 1938. In 1940 Mr. Hearst got rid of his airplane, and Allen went into the Air Force. Mr. Hearst wrote a letter of recommendation for Allen when he left. Mr. Hearst wrote about him as a pilot, "He is not only the most skillful, in my range of knowledge, but the wisest. He has taken me through many difficult situations, but better than that, he has kept me out of many. He is leaving me because I have given up my plane." Allen made lieutenant colonel in the Air Force and received the Distinguished Flying Cross.

After World War II, Allen returned as Mr. Hearst's pilot. The new plane, a DC-3C built by Douglas, had a large entrance door, a modified cargo door. The first time Mr. Hearst walked inside the plane he said, "This is the only plane I have ever entered without having to remove my hat." Mr. Hearst often wore a hat.

Besides Allen's wife Billie, who served as the hostess on the plane, three other employees worked at the airport. Gene Guthnecht was the bookkeeper and general organizer. Russ Clark, the mechanic, had a fully equipped workshop. Kendall Benedict, "Benny", the copilot, a tall, good looking young man, furnished the entertainment at the airport. Benny was a

85

Mr. Hearst's new airplane, a DC-3C, with pilot Allen Russell and hostess Billie Russell, showing the modified cargo door and the insignia designed by Allen and Billie.

paradox. This handsome copilot wanted to be a pig farmer.

Benny rented 15 acres with a house and barn on Pico Creek near the horse ranch. He strung up two wires around his pig farm to build an electric fence, and connected it to a neon light transformer, giving it very high voltage. He turned his pigs loose in the pasture. The next morning he found ten pigs all kneeling on their front legs under the bottom wire of the fence. Benny had run the bottom wire too high, and every time a pig raised up to back away from the wire, it knocked the pig down again. The pigs finally gave up and stayed kneeling under the fence.

Allen made several landings in the new airplane at night. He told us the large hay barn near the airport needed a light on top. So on February 11, 1947, Sherman Eubanks, Marks Eubanks' son, and I put a red obstruction light on top of the barn.

While we were up there putting the light on the barn, Mr. Apperson, the ranch superintendent, asked us to put in a control system to start and stop a hoist that pulled hay into the top of the barn. As an electrician, I had the opportunity to work throughout the Castle and the surrounding Hearst property, with all types of craftsmen, including cowboys. I had the privilege of seeing it all, from airport to Castle to hay barn.

This old barn fell down in the big storm of 1982 (along with the giraffe shelter). Time continues to change all the old landmarks.

On October 25, 1947 we put in lightning arresters on the airport electric service. This was the final touch, the airport was then complete.

The Airport In 1960

Thirteen years later, I came back to the airport to put in some additional lighting. Mr. Hearst was gone and many changes had taken place. What I saw sitting in the hangar was quite a shock to me. There were tractors, hay, seed grain, a bulldozer, and other farm equipment. The hangar had made a good utility shed.

The Electric Shop

The electric shop looked like a store and warehouse combined. We had a long workbench with test equipment to work on telephones and electrical apparatus. We had all the necessary tools for electrical work and power and telephone line construction.

French, magneto, and other types of phones sat in rows on a long table. Bells, buzzers, push buttons, and other switches were on one shelf. A great number of replacement switches and switch plates were kept on hand. Fuses ranged from six to 2,300 volts. And this was only part of our supply — we used an old bunkhouse on the ranch to store more materials.

Light bulbs of various colors, shapes, and sizes took up a number of shelves. When the light fixtures were first hung, Mr. Hearst chose the lamps he wanted to use in each of them, and Marks never changed the style from the original bulb.

When we got word that Mr. Hearst was coming, there was always an air of excitement for everyone, because that meant there would be guests and new activities.

The first thing I would do before Mr. Hearst arrived was go to his quarters in "A" House, take out all the light bulbs, and put in new ones. It didn't matter if the lamps were still good — I still put in new ones. We used the old lamps in the shops or construction camps. Mr. Hearst never ordered this done. It was just a courtesy, because we knew he hated to see burned out light bulbs.

The Carpenter Shop

The carpenter shop sat on a hill across the road from the indoor pool. During 1946 the shop was busy turning out work for the new wing under construction. The outside of the shop looked like an old lumber shack, but upon entering, one wished for a guide to explain all the tools and activities. The workmen never looked up from their work, as they were accustomed to frequent visitors.

Odd-shaped wooden moldings, carved faces, fancy doors, and extra pieces of carved wood hung from the ceiling beams and walls. Some of the tools were handmade to do special jobs. On the workbenches, planes with jagged blades, chisels with cupped edges, square nails, old hinges, and large wood clamps were scattered about. The cabinet drawers were full of modern and antique hardware.

Many of the workmen were skilled at fancy woodwork. Some carved wood to replace damaged pieces. They duplicated these old pieces to the extent of even drilling worm holes. Different sizes of chain were used to beat the wood to age it, since different chains left different marks. After the painter finished his work, only a skilled craftsman could tell the difference between the old and the new.

The Plumbing Shop

The plumbing shop was well equipped; it could have taken care of any small city water system. Besides the standard tools and materials in the shop, there were large dies with gears and

Marble bathroom in the new wing.

motors to turn them, and pipe wrenches so large that it usually took two men to handle them. These tools were used on the large pipeline coming from the spring to the Castle.

Smaller tools were used to install gold fixtures in the bathrooms. Many of the fancy bathtubs, washbasins, and gold fixtures were still in crates waiting to be set in the marble bathrooms.

In one corner were buckets of one-inch-square tile covered with gold leaf. This tile was used on the floor of the indoor swimming pool.

James Rankin
Plumbing Contractor

The man in charge of plumbing construction was James Rankin. Mr. Rankin could work on a dirty black boiler while wearing a suit, white shirt, and necktie, and never get dirty. He always carried a clean white rag in his hand. I would watch him work, trying to learn how he stayed so clean. I would carry a clean white rag with me just like he did, but within five minutes, the rag and I were both dirty.

Mr. Rankin was an older man. He looked like Colonel Sanders with his white hair, eyebrows, and mustache. When I talked to Mr. Rankin, I always watched his eyebrows, because all expression and emotion were shown with his eyebrows. His eyebrows showed approval, doubt, and scorn. I think Mr. Rankin invented the cliche' "to browbeat." Many times while working with him, I would catch myself arguing with his eyebrows.

Mr. Rankin and I were working on a boiler under the kitchen. I crawled under the floor of the pantry to fasten a conduit. It was dark, and I picked up a scrap of paper. When I

GUEST LIST

............................April 24,............... 193/47

"A" HOUSE

L. F.	OCCUPIED	R. F.	OCCUPIED
L. B.	"	R. B.	"
HERO	"	SHIELD	"

"B" HOUSE

L. F.	Mr. Berlin	R. F.	Mr. Haworth
L. B.	Mr. Walker	R. B.	Mr. Mitchell

"C" HOUSE

L. F.	Mr. & Mrs. David Hearst	R. F.	Mr. & Mrs. George Hearst
L. B.	Louella Parsons	R. B.	W. R. Hearst, Jr.
L. TOWER	Dunky	R. TOWER	
L. TERR.		R. TERR.	

CLOISTERS

No. 1	Princess Pignatelli	No. 3	Harry Crocker
No. 1	Stefanella	No. 3	
No. 2	Mr. Swinnerton	No. 4	
No. 2	Mrs. Swinnerton	No. 4	

CASTLE

S. DECK	OCCUPIED	N. DECK	OCCUPIED
S. DUP. U.	"	N. DUP. U.	"
S. DUP. L.	"	N. DUP. L.	"
S. CEL.	Janet Feck	N. CEL.	Ethel Whitmire
S. DOGES		N. DOGES	

1st Floor Over Billiard Room	GOTHIC
2nd Floor Over Billiard Room	Mr. & Mrs. MacKay
3rd Floor Over Billiard Room	

Guest list dated April 24, 1947.

94

MENU

La Cuesta Encantada, ✦ San Simeon, California

Luncheon December 11, 1945

SALAD

LAMB STEW & DUMPLINGS

MASHED TURNIPS   BOILED POTATOES

FRUIT   ICE

****

DINNER

OYSTER CRAB IN PATTY SHELLS

CURRIED CHICKEN & RICE

BUTTERED STRING BEANS

LEMON MERINGUE   ICE

****

"COLORADO PIONEERS"   REPUBLIC

BILL ELLIOTT   BOBBY BLAKE

NEWSREEL   MGM EXCHANGE

Breakfast 9:00 to 12:00   Luncheon 2:00   Dinner 9:00

Old menu dated December 11, 1945, with theatre program.

saw it in the light, it was a guest list dated April 24, 1947. Among the names on it was Louella Parson's name.

Mr. Rankin finished his work on the boiler and was sweeping the floor. He used a piece of heavy paper for a dustpan, and then threw it and the dirt into the trash can. I picked this paper out of the trash can to use as my dustpan. It was an old menu dated December 11, 1945. On the back of it was typed: "It is requested that the items in this cupboard not be used for room service or removed for any other purpose by unauthorized person or persons inasmuch as these articles are personal property of Mr. Hearst. This includes all of the silverware, china, etc."

I put the old menu under my shirt so as not to fold it, and took the menu and guest list home to show my wife, Joyce, not knowing that someday they would become collector's items.

Val George
And
The Blacksmith Shop

Val George, the iron worker, had charge of the blacksmith shop. I often thought the blacksmith shop looked like Val, sort of like a dog and its master. Val was a small man and walked with a limp. I never knew why he limped; he never told me and I never asked. Watching Val work was as if he was all hands, and his small torso only served the purpose of holding his hands together. If Val was asked if he could fix or make something, he would respond, "If someone else has made it, I can make it." Val had a great self-concept. Val used to tell me to never let design supersede function. Those who do are dishonest, except for artists.

Val had made many of the tools in the shop. He had a forge, an anvil, tongs to handle red hot iron, benders, jigs, and all types and sizes of hammers. Some of his tools are now on display at the Castle.

He could take red hot iron and shape it into a leaf, a flower, or whatever the situation required. He made fire screens, grills, iron gates, and many of the hand rails in the Castle.

At the entrance to the ranch, about one-half mile north of the Visitor's Center on Highway 1, is a sign which reads, "Piedras Blancas Ranch". The letters are surrounded with a cowboy on horseback, cows, and pine trees. This sign was the last thing Val made before he left the Castle. Val was small in stature, but one of the biggest men I have ever known.

Old entrance to the ranch with the sign made by Val George.

New entrance to the ranch.

The Casting Shop

The old casting shop, behind the Castle and down the hill, was where the cement and plaster casts were made. On the floor were wooden molds waiting for plaster to be poured into them. Much of the work was done by hand. Large hoes had two holes in them for mixing mortar.

The shop was also used to store materials. Overall, it looked like an accumulation of back-breaking work.

The Dump

The dump, just over the hill from the casting shop, was where broken pieces and mistakes were discarded. Once I looked over this dump with all its broken pieces, heads, arms, parts of a lion, broken tools, pipe, and scraps from every craft. Someone had dumped wet plaster, sticking many of these pieces together. It looked like a surrealistic piece of art that Salvador Dali might have made.

An old cement mixer stood at the edge of the dump. It had cables fastened to a large scoop to dump the sand and cement into the mixer.

All of these pieces in the dump I tried to identify as to what they were and their relation to the Castle. I could then understand the feelings of an archaeologist at a dig.

The Old Powerhouse

In the early construction of the Castle, there was no electricity. Coal oil lanterns were used for light. Then Mr. Hearst had a powerhouse and water wheel generator installed. The powerhouse was built in 1921, southwest of the Castle, in a little valley where it could not be seen from the highway or the Castle.

The generator inside of the powerhouse put out 2300 volts and was turned with a vertical gasoline engine manufactured by Standard Gas Engine Company at 120 horsepower, 4 cycle, 320 R.P.M., connected to the generator by direct drive. The gasoline engine and generator cost approximately $12,300.00.

A water wheel with another generator, which also put out 2300 volts, was built along a stream fifty yards from the powerhouse. A pipe carried water to the water wheel from the upper reservoir, creating good water pressure. The formula for figuring the power output of the water wheel was: number of cubic feet per minute (times) effective head (times) 62.3 pounds (divided by) 33,000 (equaled) the output. Miss Julia Morgan and her engineers used this formula to figure the size of the water wheel.

At midnight, the operator would shut down the gasoline generator and the water wheel took over the small general lighting load.

Marks operated the old powerhouse. On June 21, 1922, when Marks and Hazel Eubanks were married, no house was available for them in San Simeon, so they spent their honeymoon in the old powerhouse.

In 1928 the powerhouse was shut down. This marked the end of an era.

The old powerhouse, taken in 1921. The vent on the top is for the gasoline engine.

Power Brought
To The Castle

In 1928 PG&E brought in their first power lines to the Castle, the ranch, and the town of San Simeon. At Pico Creek, near the horse ranch, a master meter and transformers were installed. This supplied the ranch and San Simeon with a 2300 volt line. The voltage drop was so bad, however, that instead of 115 volts, sometimes it would be as low as 95 volts.

An 11,000 volt line ran from the horse ranch to the Castle with another large meter at the Castle. The first month's electric bill in 1928 was $1,315.96, and in 1945 for the month of April the electric bill for the Castle was $1,603.91. Mr. Hearst also paid the electric bill for San Simeon and the ranch.

On July 16, 1939, the old water wheel and its generator were sold for scrap. The powerhouse generator and gasoline engine were sold for scrap in 1949.

In 1947 PG&E renewed their old lines by installing new lines, and we then tore down all the old original lines to San Simeon, the ranch, and the Castle.

The Powerhouse
Building Torn Down

In 1952 Mr. Apperson, the ranch superintendent, gave me the old powerhouse building, if I would remove it. It was built of brick and I wanted this building for the used brick.

My sons, Lynn and Mike, and I with the help of Bill Sewell, the high school coach, cleaned and hauled all of the used brick from this building.

Six beautiful porcelain tube insulators ran through the double brick wall. Three small insulators protected the wires coming from the water wheel generator, and three large insulators protected the wires going to the Castle.

I kept one large and one small insulator and had a lamp made from them. The large insulator holds a copper bowl for oil and a wick. The small insulator serves as the handle. They are fastened together with a wide copper band. It made an unusually beautiful old lamp. My son, Mike, has it in his home in Cambria. The lamp is all that is left of the old powerhouse and the water wheel.

104

The old powerhouse being torn down in 1952. My oldest, son, Byron Lindsey Hanchett, at 12 years old is standing on the motor base.

Lamp made from tube insulators that went through the wall of the old powerhouse.

106

Learning
To Climb Poles

Power lines and telephone lines were strung all over the place, but they were well concealed. When I first went to work at the Castle, Marks asked me if I could climb poles. I told him no, but I was willing to learn. He gave me a safety belt and a set of climbers to strap on my legs, and said, "These are yours; take care of them, but do not sharpen the climbers until you learn more about them."

He then took me through the wild animal compound. We got out of his car, and Marks rolled the windows up about half way. He left Dynamite, his little dog, in the car. He said, "I have to roll the windows up to keep Dynamite from chasing all the wild animals." We walked over to a small, hard, creosote pole, twenty-five feet tall. The pole was standing on top of a cliff over a canyon about 100 feet down.

Marks started explaining to me how to climb. He said, "There are two main things to remember when climbing a pole. First, you always climb the high side of a pole." I asked, "What's the high side?" He said, "If the pole leans to the south, you climb the north side." He paused, making sure I understood. Then he emphasized, "And second, always keep your butt away from the pole." He walked out from under the pole for his own safety, which didn't give me much confidence, and added, "Don't burn the pole." I thought to myself, I'm not going up any pole that fast!

I had trouble sticking my spikes into that hard little pole. I got just about to the top when I looked down the cliff. It just added another 100 feet to the height of the pole. It was like climbing a pole 125 feet high. So I got a little closer to the pole. Then it happened. My spurs slipped out and I slid all the way down the pole. Marks rushed over from his safety zone and asked, "Are you all right?" I never answered. I unfastened my safety belt from the pole and checked to see if I could still walk. As I dropped my pants to pick the creosote slivers out of my legs, stomach, and various other places, I said to him, "Well, I learned one thing, and that is what you meant by burning a pole." Marks laughed and said, "Yes, you do that real well." "Now," he said, "You should get up and go right back up that pole." I asked him, "Is it all right if I pick these slivers out first?"

After picking out the slivers, I started up the pole again. This time, I did not look down the cliff, and I kept my butt away from the pole. I climbed to the top and back down. Marks put his hand on my shoulder and said to me, "If you can climb that hard little pole on the cliff, you can climb any of them." Then he added, "There are some square poles that run from the ranch house to the poultry ranch." With that, he ended the sentence, leaving me with square poles to worry about.

Years later, as I rode up and down the hill, I would look down at that little hard pole and smile to myself.

108

The Old Power Lines

In 1949, PG&E finished running their new power lines from the horse ranch to the Castle. Marks and I contracted on our own time to take down the old power lines. The Hearsts gave us eighty percent of the copper, and our share came to $1,326.12.

Ralph Jensen, one of my co-workers, and I were taking down all the old lines in San Simeon. We would push a knife blade into the bottom of the pole. If it was rotten, we pushed it over. If it was solid, we climbed the pole and untied the wires to salvage the pole.

One day, we were working near the town hall in San Simeon where they were having a meeting and cars were parked all around. I saw George Hearst's car parked at the front door. Ralph and I decided to wait until the meeting was over before taking down any more poles, and it was a good thing we did. After the last car pulled away, Ralph went up a solid pole and untied the wires. When he untied the last wire, two poles further down the line fell over. One pole with a transformer on it fell through the roof of the town hall, even making a hole in the floor. Transformer oil was all over everything. We told Marks what happened and he had the roof and floor patched and the oil cleaned up.

Later, George Hearst came down to where Ralph and I were working. He said to us, "You fellows missed me." He laughed, "I'm glad you waited to take that pole down. I'd rather have a hole in the building than in my head."

Wild Animal Compound

Sometimes the telephone lines from the Castle to San Simeon would get crossed, and it was my job to walk these lines and correct the trouble. These phone lines also ran through the wild animal compound, which consisted of some 2,000 acres, surrounded by about ten miles of fence along the perimeter. The fence was eight feet high and made of heavy wire with a four-inch mesh. The fence was buried eighteen inches into the ground, so predators could not dig underneath to harm the young animals. Marks gave me instructions how to walk the phone line in the animal compound. He told me to keep the climbers on my legs and to throw rocks at any animals between me and the next pole. The ostriches were the ones I feared the most. One had attacked a man on the road who had left his car and hurt him badly.

Marks related a story to me. One time, he was up one of these poles, and a large bull elk came over and racked his horns on the bottom of the pole. During rutting season, some of these bull elks can become very stubborn. Marks climbed down the

110

pole a ways and threw his pliers at the elk. He missed the elk, so he came down a little lower and took the test phone off his shoulder, which was in a leather case with a shoulder strap. He held onto the strap and hit the elk with the phone. He broke the phone and couldn't call for help, so he had to stay up there until the elk went away.

I enjoyed walking this phone line because there was always so much to see. The animals were all herbivorous. I would see water buffalo, yak, emu, ostriches, elk, eland, tahr goats, white deer, spotted deer, sambar deer, kangaroos, barbary sheep, zebra, and llamas. At one time, this was the largest privately-owned animal collection in the world.

An animal shelter in the compound.

John Conally was in charge of the animals. Carey Baldwin, who held that position before John, was put in charge of the animals at the San Francisco Zoo after he left the Castle.

When John fed the animals, he would string out the hay in

Buffalo herd.

long rows so the smaller animals would have a chance to eat. A hundred yards of animals would all be lined up eating and, like chickens, they had their pecking order. They chased each other from one spot to another.

Animals at feeding time.

Various kinds of animals eating together.

When I walked this phone line, I watched out for poison oak as well as animals. One day, while walking through the animal area, I found an abandoned emu nest. The two large black eggs were a little smaller than ostrich eggs. I took them home and added them to my game bird egg collection from the poultry ranch. It sure looked strange with emu eggs on one end and quail eggs on the other.

In 1928 a construction worker ran into an emu on the road to the Castle and killed it. Mr Hearst was very upset and imposed a strict speed limit through the compound.

Another interesting place in the compound was the bone yard. Any animal that died was dragged to the bone yard. I always walked through there to look at all the unusual heads and horns. If I found a good set of horns, I would carry them down the hill with me. John Conally told me how to fix these horns by shining them with brown shoe polish, and they came out beautifully.

Sometimes while walking, I would see animals fighting.

Two emu in the compound.

The barbary sheep put on quite a show. They would back up and run, cracking their heads together. One sheep would lower his head a little more than the other one, scraping his horns across his opponent's face, and this would usually end the fight.

Llamas leading the truck to the feeding area.

114

The most vicious fight I ever saw was between two llamas. Llamas are such peaceful-looking animals, one would never think they would be such vicious fighters. When fighting, two male llamas try to render each other sexless. They rear up on their hind legs, get on their knees, and go through all kinds of contortions. The things I saw were always worth the walk.

The largest camel. The tree in the background seems to add to his size.

More camels.

A young giraffe being tamed.

Exercising The Animals

Ralph Jensen and I had a way to exercise the animals. We had an old Model A flatbed truck. In the mornings, the truck was loaded with materials and tools, and we went down the hill to work. On the way down, I drove and Ralph would put his arm out the window and pick oranges to eat. Ralph would also pick kumquats from a kumquat tree that grew along the road. These kumquats were sour and small and just the right sizes to shoot in a sling shot we had made.

As we came into the wild animal compound, he would shoot the sheep, goats, and deer with the kumquats, and I would turn the key to the truck on and off, making it backfire. It would sound like a shot gun. Goats and sheep would fly off the rocks. Deer and eland would jump over each other and run and chase each other. They actually seemed to enjoy a good run. Anytime the animals heard this truck come down the hill, the whole compound came alive.

When we came back up the hill, Marks would say, "You guys ought to fix the muffler on that truck. You're scaring those

animals to death." Ralph and I would just look at each other
and smile.

Marks Eubanks repairing the old work truck.

The Polar Bears

On the downhill road leaving the Castle, one can see a large concrete area on a hillside near the road. The polar bears were kept there. The polar bear pits were constructed in January of 1932. This location was chosen because there was plenty of room and it was cooler on this side of the hill. The story is told that ice was hauled in for them on hot days.

The polar bear pits.

The Great Ape

Many stories have been written about the Castle and its surroundings and activities. Some of these articles were taken out of context — the context of life. A good example was a story written by Robert Jennings, August 24, 1969, in *West Magazine,* a supplement to the *Los Angeles Times.* The article was quoting Ilka Chase, who wrote about the large ape in the zoo, "This great ape gripped the bars and screamed in frenzy whenever he caught sight of Mr. Hearst." Well, I have news for Ilka Chase and Mr. Jennings. This was not all that ape would do — some things are unprintable.

They did not tell the whole story, however. It was not only Mr. Hearst that the ape hated — he hated everyone. The reason was that the construction workers teased him and made him mean. Mr. Hearst eventually gave him to the zoo in San Francisco because he said the ape was not happy here.

The animal cages for the zoo were completed in 1925. In 1928 it cost Mr. Hearst $300 a month to feed the animals. From all I have heard, I don't think Mr. Hearst was too happy with having the animals caged in the zoo. The zoo cages were torn down in 1949 by my friend, Noel Williams.

Norman Johnson
And
The Dog Kennels

Norman Johnson was called "the Dog Man". He had a small room with a bath near the dog kennels. Norman was in charge of the dogs.

On Elephant Hill, near the kennels, he had a large walk-in refrigerator room to keep meat for the dogs. Another room was used to grind and cook the dog food. I spent a lot of time repairing his large hot plates. He was forever letting the dog food boil over.

In April of 1966, I wrote Mr. Johnson a letter asking for information to put in my scrapbook. He answered my letter, which I would like to share with you:

May 5, 1966

Dear Byron,

> *Yes, I do remember you very well, and I am rather surprised to hear you are now employed by the State doing electrical work up there. It was nice hearing from you, and will try to get together some kind of letter with the information you asked for.*
> *I came to the hilltop in the spring of 1932 to work*

*with the animals, and had charge of the elephant
and a small number of dogs, which was the start of
one of the finest and largest kennels in this country.
When we closed the kennels in October of 1951, upon
Mr. Hearst's passing away, we had about ninety
dogs, mostly Dachshunds, long and short-haired, as
we favored this breed above all others, and during
my time up there from spring of 1932 to October of
1951, he always had a smooth-haired Dachshund as
a pet. In fact, he had only two different dogs in all
those years. The first one, Helen, died in his arms of
some complication at his place at Wyntoon,
California. I had a daughter of Helen at the kennel,
named Helena, so she was elected to replace Helen.
Helena lasted the rest of Mr. Hearst's life.*

*A few of the other breeds we had in our kennels at
times were Kerry Blue Terriers, Boston Bulls,
Sheepdogs, and Heuleguin Danes. We probably
raised as many as 150 more puppies, which increased
the number of dogs in our kennels so fast, as we did
not give many away. His newspaper officials were
mostly on the list with a few motion picture celebs,
and he always wanted to be sure the dogs would get a
good home.*

*The dog kennels with the zoo on the left in the background, now
called Elephant Hill.*

122

I used close to 500 lbs. of dog biscuits (nutro) a month and for meat we fed mostly beef, mostly culls from the ranch, a couple beefs a week and also, occasionally, we fed deer meat from an over-populated herd on the hilltop.

I ground about 40 lbs. of meat, cooked this, and then added the meat and soup to the biscuits. I would alternate on feeding bones and would leave enough meat on the bones to take the place of the other feed for that day. The dogs used milk in the morning.

I have not mentioned Miss Davies' dog, Ghandi, who also was a Dachshund. When Mr. Hearst and Miss Davies would go abroad, their dogs were always left in my care at the kennels. I would receive several nice woolen blankets for their dogs to sleep on. On their return from abroad, they would wind up probably in Wyntoon or Santa Monica, and whichever place it would be, I would have to take their pets to them. We traveled first class with a state room, so the dogs would not have to be crated.

Byron, there were so many interesting happenings that I could go on for hours writing about them, and so many humorous things. Hope this will be of value to your scrapbook. We both wish you well and happiness on your job.

Norman and Margaret

Norman's letter told his story much better than I could.

Norman Johnson and his elephant, Mary Ann; taken in 1932.

The Horse Ranch

The horse ranch is located south of the Castle, near Highway 1 on Pico Creek.

In 1947 new fences were built. The water system was improved with a large wooden tank supplied by two wells. The ranch house, apartments, stables, and tack room were remodeled and rewired. Feed grinders, mixers, and metal tanks to hold the feed were installed.

The tack room had beautiful saddles and other unusual gear. Some of the saddles showed use and were strictly western; others were definitely for show.

The Hearst boys were interested in the horse ranch. They flew in Arabian horses for breeding stock.

When these new horses arrived, Buck Dyer, the manager, had me wire in a dark room, so pictures and records could be kept on every horse.

One old stallion on the ranch belonged to Mr. Hearst. This old stallion was given special treatment, like an old retired gentleman.

Cowboy Lloyd Jung with one of the Arabian horses on the horse ranch.

Cambria has a Pinedorado celebration and parade every year. One Year, Bill Hearst, Jr. was chosen as Grand Marshall. He rode one of these Arabian stallions in the parade. Bing Crosby was his guest and rode with him. Bing and Bill, with the stallion, were an interesting addition to the parade.

Buildings On The Ranch

The next project was wiring and rewiring the old ranch house, cowboy bunkhouse, office, barns, and other buildings on the ranch.

The beautiful old Phoebe Apperson Hearst ranch house.

Every ranch house in the 1800's always had an orchard with a variety of fruit trees. This old Phoebe Apperson Hearst home was no different; it also had an orchard. Native deer often stayed under the trees eating the apples.

The flower garden in the yard covered a large area with a footbridge crossing a creek. In addition to my work on the house, I put in a greenhouse electrically heated to raise flowers.

Several of the things I remember inside the ranch house were the unusual tile areas over the openings of each fireplace. And at the top of the stairway hung a fancy Mexican saddle.

The cellar under the house looked like a museum. One day my helper and I discovered two barrels sitting on a brick ledge and, upon exploring them, we found they contained bottles of beer packed in straw. We decided to sample a bottle; it tasted terrible. My helper said, "I didn't know beer aged in glass, but this sure has."

On one of the shelves was an old mason jar full of fruit that had turned dark in color. We wondered if this fruit came from the old orchard.

While under the beautiful old house, I found an old newspaper pushed over the top of a floor joist brace. It was the *San Francisco Examiner,* dated Tuesday morning, June 7, 1898. This newspaper contained interesting articles written about the war with Spain and the sinking of the Battleship Maine. Some of the advertisements were:

Horse hides .... *$1.50 each*
Colt hides .... *50¢ each*
Honey .... *10¢ pound*
Eggs .... *16¢ dozen*
Sugar-cured hams ... *10¢ pound*
Beef .... *6-¼¢ pound*
Veal .... *5-½¢ pound*

Lamb	*8¢ pound*
Hogs	*6¢ pound*
Gasoline in bulk	*20¢ gallon*

Across the road from the office was a large barn. The hay was kept in the large center area, and on each side were stalls for the work horses. One wall of this barn, which was 80 feet long, was covered with horse harnesses, bridles, and collars, all hanging on their separate pegs. Marks told me that these harnesses had been on the horses pulling materials up the hill to build the Castle. In March 1924, Mr. Hearst wrote to Julia Morgan instructing her to buy more work horses to work on the Castle construction. It must have been an interesting sight in the early morning to see all the horses lined up being harnessed.

Horse harness hanging in the old barn on the ranch.

After exploring the old barn, we started with the wiring. On the front peak of the barn we installed a 1,000 watt floodlight; one from the old airport hangar. We put the switch for this light in the superintendent's office, across the road from the barn. In those days, this was the only road leading to the Castle, and there were no tours, but plenty of curious tourists.

The ranch office.

Next to the office we put in a power pole with a siren on top. This served the ranch and Castle in any emergency to combine manpower. It was used mostly for brush and grass fires.

Cipriano Soto
Western Gentleman

Cipriano Soto was born in 1870 and had worked on the Hearst ranch since he was 17 years old. He dressed western, not as a cowboy, but as a western gentleman. He was a wiry old man with a full, well-trimmed mustache. The brim of his hat was always just the right width to match his size and the features of his face, and he wore his hat at just a little angle, which added to the alertness of his dark eyes. The first time anyone saw Cipriano, they would always take a second look.

Cipriano had many stories to tell and I loved to listen to them. The first time I met him, we were at the old dairy barn on the ranch. He called me over to the old barn and said to me, "Come with me, I want to show you something." I followed him into the barn. He pointed to an old coach covered with dust and spider webs saying, "I used to drive this coach. I was the coachman for Mrs. Hearst." He reached down with his hand and dusted off the name plate, which read "made by Studebaker," and added, "That was when the name Studebaker meant something." As we stood there, it was like he

131

was loving the old coach with his hands. He said, "I drove for Mrs. Phoebe Apperson Hearst, Mr. W. R. Hearst's mother. That was a long time ago."

FIESTA GRAND MARSHAL . . . Cipriano Soto, 78, San Simeon, born at the old San Antonio Mission on Mexican Independence day, Sept. 16, 1870, is grand marshal of the 20th annual Fiesta de las Flores parade Saturday morning. He will be riding a handsome stallion from the famed Hearst ranch, bedecked in the silver trappings for which the Hearst stable is world famed. Soto has worked for the Hearst ranch since he was 17 years old. H e was coachman for Mrs. Phoebe Hearst, mother of William Randolph Hearst, taking her to and from San Simeon and San Luis Obispo many times in coach and four. (McLain photo)

Cipriano Soto.

Four generations of Sotos have worked here at the ranch and Castle: Cipriano, Ernest, Vernon, and Bobby. Bobby, Cipriano's great grandson, is the fourth generation and is now working at the Castle on restoration.

The Horse Stable

I was repairing a telephone line at the stable when Cipriano was there. He took care of the stable when guests came to the Castle. Horses were brought to the stable, gentle horses from the cow ranch and spirited horses from the horse ranch.

Cipriano was saddling the horses and he still had plenty of talk. He said, "My biggest problem is giving the right horse to the right person." He tightened the cinch on a horse saying, "Everyone thinks they are a cowboy. I have no trouble with the Hearst boys or Miss Austine; they get along with horses." Miss Austine is the wife of Bill Hearst, Jr., Cipriano mumbled, "I can trust these horses; it's some of the people I can't trust." I had to go to work, so I left. As I went out the door, Cipriano was still talking to the horses about the people.

The Ranch Bunkhouse

Many of the cowboys and ranch hands stayed at the bunkhouse. Each had a private room and they ate in a large dining room. Whenever I worked at the ranch or airport I ate at the bunkhouse also.

The ranch bunkhouse.

One time while eating at one of the long tables in the dining room, I dropped a spoon. I slid my chair back and leaned under the table to retrieve the spoon. I was amazed at the feet under this table. There were cowboy boots with spurs on them, cowboy boots with cow manure on them, shoes splashed with cement, shoes soaked with cutting oil, and painters' shoes with various colors of paint. I could tell which pair of shoes belonged to Bill Krenkel, the equipment operator, because Bill never wore any socks.

There was quite a cross section of craftsmen seated at this table. As I raised from under the table, watching them eat, I thought the animals aren't the only ones well taken care of on this ranch.

Feeding
The Native Deer

Wells were drilled north of the Castle near Piedras Blancas Lighthouse near Highway 1 to water alfalfa for the cattle. When I installed the pump motors, I covered the motors with screen wire to keep the pack rats and field mice from building nests in them.

At one time deer were eating a large part of the alfalfa, and the ranch superintendent asked Mr. Hearst if he could shoot the deer to be rid of them. Mr. Hearst asked, "How much are they eating?" The superintendent told him they were eating all 25 acres. Mr. Hearst's answer was, "Well, there's plenty of land here. Clear off another 25 acres and plant it for the deer."

The Cowboy Camps

Marks and I had to travel into the back country, about 20 miles behind the Castle. We were wiring the cowboy camps so that a portable generator could be used to provide electricity for the cowboys to read by or play poker.

In the mornings, we loaded our materials in a jeep and drove from the Castle to the camps. One morning we chased a coyote down the road until it ran into the brush. Then we talked to Charlie Villa, a cowboy rounding up cattle.

I thought, where else in the world could one have breakfast in a Castle, talk to John Bullard about planting a rose at one of the cowboy camps, chase a coyote, and see a cowboy rounding up cattle. This was an excellent example of the variety of activities there.

The cowboy camps were named Burnett, Davis, Harris, and Tobacco. At one time, some of these places were old homesteads.

The Harris place had a small log cabin with a fireplace. This cabin was the best constructed and the neatest I had ever seen. I studied the joints where the logs met at the corners; they fit perfectly. Behind the cabin, an old hayrake sat in the center of the field. It was probably used by Mr. Harris. I would love to have known this man.

While we wired the cabin at Burnett, Archie Soto, the foreman, took me to a place where the cowboys were working. They were using a large iron kettle filled with a smelly liquid in which to dip the calves to kill the ticks and other parasites. Archie told me that this kettle was used in San Simeon years ago to boil whale oil. At one time, three of these kettles were on the ranch. One of these old kettles is now on display at the visitor's center.

At the Castle or on the ranch, interesting items of art and history were abundant for those who took the time to look around.

The Poultry Ranch

They raised chickens, turkeys, ducks, chukars, guinea hens, cornish hens, pheasants, quail, and other game birds at the poultry ranch. These birds were raised for Mr. Hearst and his guests.

All the eggs were hatched in incubators, and then the small chicks were placed in brooders. The young birds were then moved to heated rooms until they were mature.

In the winter of 1946, a big freeze hit. This caused all the heaters to operate at once, putting an overload on the electric system, which caused a power failure. They lost all the eggs in the incubators and all the small birds in the brooders.

Taylor Dillon, the manager of the poultry ranch, subsequently told Mr. Hearst of the power failure and the loss of the birds. Mr Hearst had us completely rewire the poultry ranch. He said, "If anyone is going to raise animals of any kind, they must take care of them."

By July of 1947, we had put in new power lines and transformers and rewired every building on the poultry ranch.

An alarm system was installed to warn if another power failure occurred.

A new method of raising chickens and producing more eggs began in 1946. Individual wire cages housed each bird and, in their lifetimes, their feet never touched the ground. Many of these cages were installed, and lights burned at night to encourage them to lay more eggs. One room had feed mixers and grinders. Another room was equipped to pluck and clean chickens. A large walk-in refrigerator room was used for storage. Completed in 1947, it was a large and very modern plant.

At the end of each day, Mr. Dillon would give me all kinds of unfertile game bird eggs. My three children and I had an interesting egg collection, including the two large emu eggs.

The Dairy
And Vegetable Garden

The dairy consisted of prize Jersey cows. The dairy supplied milk, butter and cheese not only to the Castle, but to all the families that lived in San Simeon. A large supply of cheese was also shipped out by boat.

Mr. Hearst never had trouble finding men to feed and milk the cows. However, he often had trouble upgrading the herd and finding someone to keep records on them.

With all the fruit trees, beef cattle, and the dairy, I often wondered if Mr. Hearst had a vegetable garden. Yes, he did. Pete Sebastian told me that his father took care of a large vegetable garden, located on the horse ranch.

The Castle was indeed self-sufficient; it had everything.

The dairy barn.

The Telephone System

The main part of the telephone system in the telephone office was completed in December of 1927. Telephone maintenance was a big job. There were actually three different systems integrated into the switchboard at the telephone office.

Byron Hanchett in 1983 with the old PBX board — the same equipment he worked on in 1946.

The Castle and grounds used eighty phones. Long distance calls could be connected to any one of these phones through the telephone office. San Simeon and the ranch had a two-wire, metallic, magneto system with a hand crank. With these magneto phones, coded long and short signals were used to call different parties. The ranch and San Simeon had thirty-six magneto phones, making a total of 116 phones. A telephone junction was located at the ranch office, and from this junction a grounded system using only one wire ran twenty miles behind the Castle to the old dairy and all the cowboy camps.

The telephone office was a center of activity. Three operators stayed at the Castle, rotating shifts so that one of them was on duty at all times. The operators were a great source of information. They knew who was coming and going, and they even controlled the airport lights.

For additional communications, a teletype machine was located in Col. Willicombe's office, which was in the telephone office, and a powerful shortwave radio was located under his office. The call letters were W6GOU. This radio was used until 1939. Then, in 1940, it was disconnected and only the teletype and telephones were used. The teletype had its advantages. Messages were received for guests, and the message could be delivered later if the guest was not immediately available.

Teletype Messages

I was working under the telephone office changing some phone wires when Marks came down. A pile of trash lay under the office — empty cardboard boxes, wrapping paper, a few old magazines, and even an empty lipstick container, probably left by one of the telephone operators. Marks spread the trash around with his foot and said, "I'll send someone to clean this up. Then after you finish your work, you can haul this trash to the dump." He took the lipstick container and went up to the telephone office to speak about the trash problem.

Under the telephone office, near the shortwave radio, was a long shelf loaded with old teletype messages. Many of these old messages would fall off the shelf and be scattered about the floor, which were then swept up with the trash.

After everything was cleaned up, I took the trash to the dump. When I dumped the trash, I looked through some of the old teletype messages and picked out a few to keep for my scrapbook. One of these messages pertained to Walter Winchell and Damon Runyon, one of my favorite writers.

144

```
WXI                               SAN SIMEON,CALIF., JUNE 5, 1939.

WARD GREENE,                        (COPIES TO PUBLISHERS AND EDITORS
KING FEATURES SYNDICATE,              OF ALL HEARST SUNDAY PAPERS)
235 EAST 45 ST NEW YORK.

    I DEFINITELY WANT WALTER WINCHELL AND DAMON RUNYON IN THE EDITORIAL
OR MARCH OF EVENTS SECTION OF THE VARIOUS SUNDAY PAPERS, -- BEGINNING
WITH ISSUE OF SUNDAY, JUNE 11.

    THESE VERY EXCELLENT WRITERS DO NOT HAVE TO WRITE THEIR SUNDAY
ARTICLES ON ESPECIALLY TIMELY SUBJECTS. CONSEQUENTLY THERE IS NO
REASON WHY THE ARTICLES CANNOT BE SUPPLIED ON WEDNESDAY OR TUESDAY OR
EVEN MONDAY OF THE WEEK BEFORE SUNDAY OF PUBLICATION.

    PLEASE SEE THAT THIS IS DONE, AND THAT THE ARTICLES ARE SENT IN
AMPLE TIME FOR THIS SECTION.

    (CAPS) AND THE PUBLISHERS AND EDITORS ARE HEREBY REQUESTED TO
SEE THAT THEY GET INTO THIS SECTION. (UNCAPS)

    IF THESE GENTLEMEN WERE WRITING FOR THE COSMOPOLITAN MAGAZINE,
THEY WOULD NOT THINK IT ANY HARDSHIP AT ALL TO GET THEIR ARTICLES
IN THE EDITOR'S HANDS WEEKS IN ADVANCE.

    IF THEY WERE WRITING FOR THE AMERICAN WEEKLY, THEY WOULD HAVE TO
TURN THEM IN TWO OR THREE WEEKS IN ADVANCE.

    AND IT IS CERTAINLY NO HARDSHIP FOR THEM TO GET THEIR ARTICLES
INTO THE SUNDAY EDITOR'S HANDS A FEW DAYS IN ADVANCE.

    SO WILL YOU KINDLY SEE THAT MR. WINCHELL AND MR. RUNYON KINDLY
DO THIS.

    AND WHEN THE ARTICLES ARE RECEIVED, THE EDITORS SHOULD AND (CAPS)
MUST (UNCAPS) GET THEM INTO THIS SECTION.

    I WANT THE ARTICLES DEFINITELY PRINTED THERE, AS STATED ABOVE,
AND (CAPS) NOWHERE ELSE. (UNCAPS)

                        W. R. HEARST.
```

Teletype message — Walter Winchell-Damon Runyon.

In addition, many of Mr. Hearst's top men referred to him as "Chief," and some of these messages refer to him by this name.

One message in particular showed the powerful influence Mr. Hearst had in the movie industry. Regarding the Warner

Bros. picture, "The Man Who Dared," the Chief says "Commend it." It's no wonder his film cabinet was full of pictures to show.

WX2

SAN SIMEON, JUNE 21, 1939

EDITORS OF ALL HEARST PAPERS--

CHIEF INSTRUCTS TO GIVE GOOD NOTICES AND PRINT SOME PICTURES ABOUT WARNER BROTHERS PRODUCTION, "THE MAN WHO DARED."

"COMMEND IT," CHIEF SAYS-- "SAY THAT IT IS A GOOD AMERICAN PICTURE AND A RELIEF FROM THE COMMUNIST PROPAGANDA THAT WE SEE ON THE SCREEN."

J. WILLICOMBE.

501PEH

Teletype message — Warner Bros. picture, "Commend it."

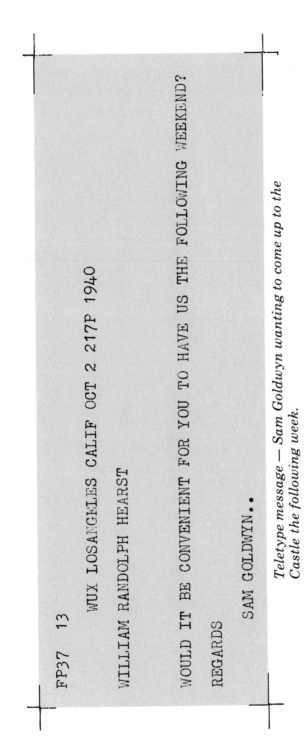

FP37 13

    WUX LOSANGELES CALIF OCT 2 217P 1940

WILLIAM RANDOLPH HEARST

WOULD IT BE CONVENIENT FOR YOU TO HAVE US THE FOLLOWING WEEKEND?

REGARDS

      SAM GOLDWYN..

Teletype message — Sam Goldwyn wanting to come up to the Castle the following week.

These teletype messages often reflected the stand Mr Hearst took on some issues. For example, he was against the abuse of animals, he was against prejudice, and he spoke out about the problems in our parole system, to name a few.

```
WX2                                 SAN SIMEON, CALIF., MARCH 17, 1939
--TO PUBLISHERS AND EDITORS
OF ALL HEARST NEWSPAPERS--
    I THINK WE SHOULD HAVE AN ENTIRELY DIFFERENT KIND OF EDITORIAL
AND CARTOON ON ST. PATRICK'S DAY THAN OUR NEWSPAPERS OR ANY NEWSPAPERS
USUALLY HAVE.
    THE EDITORIAL AND CARTOON SHOULD BE DIGNIFIED AND INSPIRATIONAL.
    WE SHOULD TREAT THE IRISH SYMPATHETICALLY AND RESPECTFULLY, AS WE
DO THE JEWS, REVIEWING A GREAT PAST AND LOOKING FORWARD TO A STILL
GREATER FUTURE.
    THEY ARE A SPLENDID RACE AND AMONG US THEY ARE ALL FINE CITIZENS.
    LET US APPRECIATE THEM, AND LET US NOT HAVE THE VAUDEVILLE IRISH
FIGURE AS A CARTOON TYPE ON ST. PATRICK'S DAY, BUT HAVE A DIGNIFIED
FIGURE OF ERIN AS WE HAVE OF COLUMBIA.
    I WAS DISTRESSED BY THE CARTOON IN SOME OF OUR PAPERS THIS ST.
PATRICK'S DAY, AND I AM SURE A GREAT MANY AMERICAN CITIZENS OF IRISH
DESCENT WILL NOT LIKE THE TONE AND CHARACTER OF IT.
                                        W. R. HEARST.
```

Teletype message — St. Patrick's Day.

WX7

SAN SIMEON, CALIF., JUNE 12, 1939.

WREN, S.F. EXAMINER,

ETTELSON, S.F. CALL BULLETIN,

HOFFMAN, OAKLAND POST ENQUIRER,

VAN ETTISCH, L.A. EXAMINER.

CAMPBELL, L.A. HERALD EXPRESS.

PLEASE CONTINUE THE FIGHT ON THE USE OF THALLIUM SULPHATE TO KILL

SQUIRRELS AND FIELD RODENTS, WHICH IS A MENACE TO HORSES, CATTLE,

DOGS AND HUMAN BEINGS.

W. R. HEARST.

PDS.

Teletype message — poisoning of animals.

149

WX5

SAN SIMEON, APRIL 1, 1938.

MEMORANDUM FOR--

MR. WREN, SF EXAMINER

MR. ETTELSON, SF CALL BULLETIN

MR. HOFFMAN, OAKLAND POST ENQUIRER

MR. VAN ETTISCH, LA EXAMINER

MR. CAMPBELL, LA HERALD EXPRESS.

CHIEF INSTRUCTS TO TELL ALL THE CALIFORNIA PAPERS TO SUPPORT THESE

ANTI-COCK FIGHTING BILLS AND "GET THAT DISGRACEFUL PROCEEDING STOPPED."

"IT IS EVEN MORE IMPORTANT," CHIEF SAYS, "TO SUPPORT THE PAROLE

HEARINGS AND AN EFFECTIVE MODIFICATION OF THE SYSTEM THAT TURNS SO MANY

CONVICTS LOOSE UPON THE COMMUNITY ON PAROLE TO RE-COMMIT THEIR

CRIMES."

J. WILLICOMBE

855PF

Teletype message — parole board, cock fighting.

150

```
WX7
                      SAN SIMEON, CALIF., JUNA 4, 1939.
E. W. COCHRANE,
   CHICAGO AMERICAN.
   (COPIES TO ALL PUBLISHERS OF ALL HEARST PAPERS)
   THINK WE SHOULD NOT ONLY ELIMINATE PRELIMINARY PROMOTION OF LOW
SPORTS LIKE PRIZE FIGHTING AND WRESTLING, BUT SHOULD MINIMIZE PICTORIAL
PRESENTATION OF EVENTS IN THESE SPORTS OF MORONS.
   I THINK BRUTAL PICTORIAL DISPLAYS GENERALLY DISGUSTING AND DISCRE-
DITING.
       W. R. HEARST.
          807PDS.
```

Teletype message — prize fighting and wrestling.

WX2

SAN SIMEON, CAL., JUNE 11, 1939.

EDITORS ALL HEARST MORNING PAPERS

AND AFTERNOONS WHERE NO MORNINGS--

CHIEF HAS REQUESTED CHICAGO HERALD EXAMINER TO SEND YOU THREE COLUMN

MATS OF CARTOON ON AUTO RACE DEATHS THAT APPEARED IN DOUBLE COLUMN

MEASURE IN THEIR ISSUE OF JUNE SIXTH. CHIEF INSTRUCTS TO PRINT THIS

CARTOON IN THREE COLUMNS, WITH THE CAPTION-- "TO MAKE A MORON HOLIDAY"

--ALTHOUGH DEEP, IT MUST BE THREE COLUMNS. ALSO CHIEF INSTRUCTS TO

PRINT WITH IT AN EDITORIAL AGAINST "THIS USELESS AND NEEDLESS SACRIFICE

OF LIFE TO PLEASE AN AUDIENCE OF MORONS AND SADISTS WHO GO THERE TO

SEE SOMEBODY KILLED."

J. WILLICOMBE.

506PEH

Teletype message — auto racing.

Cowboy Camp Phone Lines

A big brush fire in the back country burned hundreds of acres, including the neat little log cabin at the Harris place, and all the trees to which the phone line was fastened.

This phone line ran for twenty miles with only ten telephone poles, which were used to hold the lines over hay fields. All the rest of the line ran from tree to tree or tree to rock. We fastened the line to anything that was high enough, as the lines had to clear a horse and rider and the elk that were loose from the compound.

Three of us spent a month putting this line back up. We traveled by foot, by jeep, and on horseback. If I had a choice between the jeep and horseback, I took the horse. Nothing was worse than riding in a jeep with a crazy cowboy driving.

When we came to a canyon, I used a bow and arrow to shoot a small nylon line across. We tied a small rope to the nylon line to pull the wire across the canyon and over the treetops.

The halfway point on this phone line ran near the road, where we installed a telephone for use in case of an emergency.

The cowboys kept a trail cleared out under this line so we could maintain it. The guests often used this trail as a bridle path.

Byron Hanchett running telephone line to the cowboy camps.

154

Mr. Hearst's Picnic Phone

This back country had many springs and streams of water. Mr. Hearst loved this outdoor life, horses, and a picnic. He often took his guests into the back country for a picnic. In the early days, most often on horseback. In later years they all rode in cars.

He would call about a week ahead and tell us where he wanted a phone installed. I helped Marks install one of these phones in 1946. We spent two days installing it. We hung the phone under the shade of a tree, so the overhanging branches would protect it from the sun and weather.

After hanging the phone, Marks put mothballs in the battery compartment and indicated, "This keeps the wasps and yellowjackets from building nests." He laughed, "And it keeps Mr. Hearst from getting stung." As Marks closed the compartment door, he said, "I used to do this for the cowboys, but then they would never check the phone. If I leave the mothballs out, they would have to stop to clean out the yellow jackets, and then they will check the phone. It saves me a trip out here."

There is a story told that on one picnic, while the guests were sitting in the shade, one of them commented, "I wonder how the Dodgers are doing today." Mr. Hearst got up and said, "I'll go find out." He walked into a grove of trees to the phone and called one of his newspapers. He came back to his guests, gave them the score, the inning, and told them who had hit home runs. The guests wondered where he got the information out there. He loved to entertain and surprise his guests.

W.R., with his sons George and Bill, Jr., surprising their guests Western style.

The Electrical System

The electrical system was well planned, considering it was installed in the 1920's. All the switches and boxes are accessible if one knows where to find them.

Both inside and outside lighting are mostly plain lights. Few colored lights or spotlights are used for special effects. Spotlights usually tend to be a distraction because there is not just one focal point, but many.

When guests were at the Castle, Jack Doyle from the electrical staff, would spend two hours every day checking and changing light bulbs.

Whenever electrical trouble occurred, we were under floors and in attics, always looking for a way to run conduit or telephone cables. In one attic, I saw a large stone window set in place. In the process of changing and adding onto the Castle, this window had been totally enclosed inside the room.

In the Castle are two service shafts approximately two feet square. The shafts run from the lower floor to the upper floor, near the bell towers. In the shafts are many pipes; hot and cold water pipes, sewer pipes, electrical conduits, telephone cables, conduits from the old organ to the bells, and even a compressed air pipe going to the fire alarm horn on the roof between the two towers. These shafts served as a great aid in doing maintenance work or adding new wiring.

Many unusual repairs were made under the guise of electrical work. For example, two pianos were located in the assembly room, one of which was a player piano operated by an electric motor. Guests were playing this piano when the belt broke. We had no replacement, so I spliced a rope and wrapped it with friction tape, using this for a belt, so the guests could continue to play the piano. In an emergency, we improvised.

The Castle grounds at night under lights are captivating, with the trees, flowers, statues, and fountains. The lights are like makeup on a beautiful woman, with just the right amount in the right places.

However, the outside lighting was a job in itself to maintain. Some of the conduits ran under walls or tile terraces which could not be replaced. This wiring usually consisted of lead and rubber-covered wires. Over a period of years, moisture would swell the insulation, making it hard to remove the wiring from the conduit. We tried everything, including chemicals, oil, and soap, and nothing worked. Finally, Val George and I made a steam boiler and connected it to the conduit, boiling out the pipe. This helped us solve the problem.

Some of the outside wiring was just lead cable. Squirrels and pack rats would gnaw on the cable to wear their teeth down. One electrician suggested that we poison the critters, but Marks answered, "Don't ever use that word around here." If it was necessary to remove an animal, a box trap was used, and then the animal was taken away from the Castle and turned loose.

158

The Castle under lights.

Mr. Hearst's humane mouse trap.

Most of the outside lamp standards are marble, with a twelve-inch defusing bowl on top, so that one never noticed where one light ends and the other begins.

At the top of the steps on the south side of the terrace, near the Castle entrance, are two lamp standards with a square marble base. The bases are filled with concrete. When one base developed an electrical short, I chipped the concrete out of this base by hand, using a hammer and chisel. We were not allowed to use a jackhammer any place. The vibration could loosen the veneer and artifacts.

While chipping on this lamp base, I hit a soft spot and my chisel dropped down a ways. I thought I was through the concrete, but when I examined the hole, I found it was an old Prince Albert Tobacco can, a brand of tobacco popular in the

1920's. It still had tobacco in it, and had probably fallen out of some workman's pocket. It was like finding a time capsule.

The
Fire Alarm System

In 1947 and 1948, the fire protection was modernized, consisting of a new 1947 Dodge fire truck with a 350 gallon water capacity, fire plugs and hoses placed around the grounds, and a new fire alarm system. The State has since added smoke detectors.

The fire alarm system has seven stations, each station with a coded signal for its location. In the basement of the Castle is an air compressor, with 120 pounds of air pressure, connected to a horn on the roof between the two towers. When a signal is received, the horn blows.

The system was a challenge to install. Marks and I tried to locate each station where it would be effective, and yet avoid running conduit under statues, terraces, and sidewalks. When we could not avoid an obstacle, we drove all the conduit underneath, because to dig under a sidewalk could cause it to crack.

I installed the station near "A" House three different times. First, it was near the entrance and it distracted from the decorum. Then I put it farther away from the entrance, and this was too concealed. The third time, I mounted it on the box that holds the fire hose, which is where it is today. The State has done some work on the system, but it is still in use.

Byron Hanchett with the same fire alarm he installed three times in 1947.

Byron Hanchett in 1983 with the fire alarm he installed in 1947.

The Water Supply

The water for the Castle, the ranch, and the town of San Simeon is supplied by a spring. A pipe brings water down the mountain, running into a settling reservoir. Any silt or sand settles to the bottom, and then the water passes through a weir to measure its flow, and then into a large concrete storage reservoir. On February 20, 1948, there was 15/16 inch of water running through the weir. Norman Rotanzi, the gardener, keeps his eye on this water because it is so important to his plants.

The large concrete reservoir sits on a hill southeast of the Castle and can be seen from the Castle. At one time, plans were made for a large fountain to be put on top of the reservoir surrounded by large flood lights. This could have been seen from the Castle or the highway. The pipes were stubbed out for this, but the lights and fountain were never installed.

Mr. Rossi, the building superintendent, started running the pipe from the large reservoir to the Castle on January 16, 1924. The water from the large reservoir is then divided, running to the Castle and into another large concrete reservoir on the ranch, which supplies the ranch and San Simeon. A mud pond catches the overflow from this last reservoir. I installed a float switch in this mud pond in 1947, which controlled the

164

pump on a well at the poultry ranch. The cattle on the ranch and the yard of the old ranch house were watered by this mud pond. At one time, this mud pond was stocked with bass and it was good fishing.

The large reservoir at the Castle has a 5-inch pipe bringing water to the Castle yard, and also two 1,000 gallon copper tanks, one in each tower on top of the Castle. The water is gravity fed from the towers through the filter system supplying the Castle.

The Heating
And
Hot Water Systems

The Castle has both electric and steam heat. The theatre has both. The new wing is heated by steam from two large oil burning boilers under the servants' wing. The rest of the Castle is heated by electric heaters. At one time, 234 heaters were in use.

Hot water was a big item. It took thirty-five electric water heaters. Four of these heaters were in "A" House, four in "C" House, and two in "B" House. At one time, the connected electric load was 1,100 kilowatts.

Besides the electric water heaters, the Castle had two oil burning boilers in the basement, and coils in the large cook stove in the kitchen. Even the greenhouse had a boiler.

The
Fuel Oil System

In 1948, Mr. Rankin, the plumbing contractor, left the Castle, and all the maintenance was turned over to Marks. Water was scarce that year, and Norman Rotanzi found a water leak running out of the side of the hill near the greenhouse. Many gallons of water were being wasted, and we could not find the source of this leak.

John Harris even tasted the water. Marks looked at me and said, "I'm glad we're not below the septic tank." We all laughed at John. He smelled the water and it smelled like fuel oil. Then we knew it was coming from the kitchen stove and boiler system.

A 500 gallon oil tank is buried in the ground just outside the kitchen window. This tank supplies two boilers and the kitchen stove. The installation of the large kitchen stove and the boiler under the kitchen was started in June of 1924.

Water pressure is connected to the bottom of this oil tank. When water runs into the bottom of the tank, it floats the oil to the top, forcing it out to the two boilers and the kitchen stove. Three small valves on top of the tank are connected to pipes set at different depths in the tank. These tell how much oil is in the tank.

The water leak was coming from the bottom of this tank. In December of 1948, we replaced this tank with a new one.

166

Rewiring In San Simeon

On February 22, 1947, we started rewiring the town of San Simeon. All eighteen houses, each warehouse, the post office, town hall, schoolhouse, and Pete Sebastian's store and house, all had to be rewired and metered according to PG&E specifications.

When we started rewiring the houses in San Simeon, there were three electricians besides Marks. Two of us were younger men learning the trade, and the other one was a "boomer." He had worked all over the country and knew many short cuts and tricks of the trade.

The boomer worked hard and fast until about 2:00 P.M. Then he went to his car where he kept a large bag of screws, nuts, bolts, and other paraphernalia. He also kept a bottle in the bag, which was just another trick of the trade he had learned while booming. While the boomer was "in the bag," I worked. We agreed that if he left me alone, I would do the work. I learned a great deal working alone, and if I had any questions, I would always ask him before his "bag time."

Prior to the time of rewiring and putting in new electric meters, Mr. Hearst paid all the electric bills for the employees. We figured the average electric bill from the old meters, and it came to $8.68 per month. Mr. Hearst continued to pay this amount on the new electric bills.

The Warehouses

After the houses and store in San Simeon were wired, we started wiring the warehouses. This was like visiting an art gallery and a museum at the same time. There were spinning wheels, antique furniture, carved doors, marble columns, and numerous other interesting articles. One large crate was labeled "Old English Barn," which contained some of the numbered stones necessary to help construct the barn. Mexican saddles, some silver mounted and others done with fancy leather work, were all lined up the width of the warehouse.

Every warehouse was protected by a fire alarm. Nick Yost had his office and records in one warehouse. We wired a darkroom for Nick. He took pictures of every item in the warehouses. The photographs were then numbered and filed with their permanent records.

Climbing over the countless boxes to do my work in the warehouses, I saw more than if I was on tour. The warehouses were so interesting, I was sorry to finish my work in them.

Pete Sebastian's Store

Some people who visit the Castle never think to visit the old town of San Simeon. They are missing much of the history of this area. For example, the store in San Simeon was built in 1852 and is owned by Pete Sebastian. It is now a State Historical Monument. Pete's store and home are located on a small plot of land surrounded by the Hearst property. Mr. Hearst and Pete have been good neighbors for years.

Every time I went into his store, I would look at the boards in the floor and the ceiling and wish they could talk. I could imagine the endless stories that must have happened there over the many years.

Pete hired me to wire his old home and the store on my own time. While I was under the old store putting in the wiring, I used to push old bottles out of my way. In 1947 it wasn't popular to collect old bottles. Then, in the 1970's, workmen were under the store and they collected all the old bottles I had pushed aside.

For years, Pete's friends and customers would try to convince him to remodel his store. Some even wanted him to tear it down and build a new one. Pete would just smile at them, as if behind that smile Pete knew something they didn't. Pete did add on a little sun deck where his customers could eat outside. But Pete was smart. He kept the old store as it was. If he had listened to others, a part of history would have been destroyed.

The Old Pier

The old pier in San Simeon was built in 1878. Whalers originally used this pier. Then it was used for shipping and unloading materials and artifacts for the Castle. The pier stood between warehouses. A small railroad track ran from the pier straight out across the road from Pete Sebastian's store. This railroad had flat cars about eighteen inches high, four feet wide, and six feet long.

The last time this old pier was used was in 1946 and 1947. Abalone divers used it to unload their catch. Time had changed the use of this old pier, from whales to Castle artifacts to abalone.

The old pier was eventually torn down. Pilings were sticking up above and just below the water, endangering the bottoms of small boats. So, in July of 1949, Tom Grassine a co-worker, and I dynamited the old pilings, which had to be blown off next to their base in the sand. Some of these pilings, made from eucalyptus trees taken from a grove behind the warehouse, required twice the amount of dynamite as did the others.

The Hearst Corporation planned to give the County land for a new pier and campground. But before doing so, they wanted to be sure pilings could be driven into the bottom of the bay for a new pier. In 1949, Noel Williams and I took soundings for this new pier, after which the Hearst Corporation donated the land. After the pier was built, I ran lights on it and wired the campground.

The Hearst Boys

I must relate a story about the Hearst boys. I was in the theatre booth checking the film, getting ready to run a show for the boys and their guests. Randy and David, the twins, came into the booth. Randy said to me, "We have a reel of film. I think it's a picture of Dad. Will you run it after the other show is over?"

When I checked this film, I saw it was a silent movie with no sound track. The beginning of the film showed Mr Hearst mounting his horse on the right side. I was a country boy, I knew you milked a cow on the right side and mounted a horse on the left side, unless you were roping at a rodeo. But Mr. Hearst did not waste time with details. So I thought, maybe, he mounted on whichever side was closer. I continued to watch the picture. The next time he mounted the horse, he walked around the horse to enable him to mount on the right side. Then I knew what was wrong. Whoever rewound this film before had rewound it the wrong way, putting the left on the right and the right on the left. If the film had a sound track, I would have caught the mistake. I thought none of these city people would know the difference anyway. Well, I was wrong.

The minute the show was over, here came Randy and David. Randy asked me, "What is this business of Dad getting on the wrong side of the horse?" I explained that the film had been wound the wrong way, and they laughed. With all respect due Mr. Hearst, I rewound the film the right way, putting him on the left side of the horse, and the film back in the can.

Bunky Hearst

Bunky is Mr. Hearst's grandson, son of John Hearst. He stayed at the Castle and had his own quarters.

Bunky could associate with anyone and talk their language. He ate with the help and made many friends with construction workers and the Castle help. He got a good education from his association with the help — maybe it wasn't all good, but he got a sample of reality.

Bunky attended Cambria High School. Many times, Ann Miller or Norman Rotanzi drove him to his school activities until he got his driver's license.

Bunky Hearst and Roy Evans, the labor foreman.

172

The Two Grandsons

Starting in 1960, Mr. Bill Hearst, Jr. and his wife, Austine, sent the employees Christmas cards every year. The cards were always pictures of their two sons, Mr. Hearst's grandsons, William R. Hearst, III, and Austin Hearst.

In 1964, they got a dog, Stonewall Jackson, and he was included in the pictures, giving his paw print for his signature. In 1968, William started college, and only Austin and Stonewall Jackson were in the picture. In 1969, Austin had gone off to school, and in the picture was only Stonewall Jackson and his paw print. This was the last Christmas card. Laying the cards out in succession is like watching these boys grow up.

Here's what's inside:
Our wishes for your joy at Christmas
our hopes that the Divine Child will
bring you all blessings in 1960.
Will and Austine

William R. Hearst III
austin Hearst

1959 Christmas card from Mr. and Mrs. Bill Hearst, Jr. showing a picture of their sons, William and Austin.

The card text reads:

Our wish for you—
A bright Christmas,
A peaceful 1967,
blessings and love
from the Christ Child
always ———
Will and Austine

Will III
Austin Hearst I
*
Stonewall Jackson II

Christmas card from Mr. and Mrs. Bill Hearst, Jr. with a picture of their two boys, William and Austin, and Stonewall Jackson.

1967 finds son William off at college, leaving Austin and Stonewall Jackson to do the posing.

Austin says he won't
pose again without Willie.
Willie says he's too busy
at college—
Jackson will pose
Christmastime or anytime—
But no matter what—
we all wish you
blessings for Christmas
and 1968—
  Will and Austin—
  (Stonewall Jackson II)

Waiting for Christmas—
sending with this card (our
last one!) wishes that you
and those you love will
be blessed in 1969—
and through the years—
Will and Austine

Willie III
Austine

(Stonewall Jackson II)

The Hearst's last family Christmas card, 1968, with Stonewall Jackson doing a solo.

Assembling Toy Electric Cars

Mr. Bill Hearst, Jr., Miss Austine, and their two boys stopped me on the terrace in front of the Castle one day. She took two little electric cars and their related parts out of a box. She asked me, "Can you assemble these for us so they will run?" I saw the instruction sheet fall out of the box. As I picked it up, I said in a positive way, "Sure I can fix them." But as I unfolded the instructions, I saw they were written in German. Using trial and error, I finally got them to work. As I walked away and looked back, it seemed odd seeing two little boys running electric cars on the terrace in front of the Castle.

Candles In "A" House Light Fixture

After Mr. Hearst left the Castle, Mr. & Mrs. Bill Hearst, Jr. stayed at "A" House. Miss Austine sent word for me to come to "A" House. As I walked into the room, she was looking up at two ornate light fixtures covered with gold leaf hanging from the ceiling. She said to me, "I would like those light bulbs that hang down to be removed and placed inside the bowl of the fixture, so they will shine upwards toward the ceiling. In other words, instead of bare bulbs hanging down, there would be indirect lighting."

After I got over the shock of the job I had to do, I looked up in the direction of the two fixtures. What I was really looking for was a way to talk her out of doing it, but as she talked, I could see she knew what she wanted and how she wanted to do it. I said to her, "If you will stay and help me, I'm sure the two of us can do the job."

We reworked the fixtures. The light sockets were "dewired" and placed around the edge of the fixture. Candles were placed in the light sockets, and they looked very appropriate for the

179

decor of the room. At a much later date Miss Austine told me that the family had never lit those candles.

A light fixture in "A" House that Mrs. Bill Hearst, Jr. and Byron Hanchett changed from electricity to candle power.

Christmas At The Castle

Christmas was a happy time at the Castle. On Friday, December 20, 1946, I decorated Mr. Hearst's Christmas tree in "A" House. Mr. Hearst left instructions for me to leave extra tinsel so Miss Davies could put some on the tree. Well, I did better than that — I left extra tinsel, and I also left a little bare spot on the tree for her to decorate.

The Refectory decorated for Christmas dinner; date unknown.

Every Christmas, all the employees got a Christmas check. One Christmas, John Harris, the prankster, started a rumor with a whispering campaign. A few days before Christmas, John whispered a secret to one of the old gardeners, "Mr. Hearst is going to give everyone a turkey for Christmas. Don't tell anyone." Before the day was over, everyone was talking about the turkey, and John gave the men two days to carry the news home and make plans with their wives.

The next day, one of the gardeners said to John, "Isn't it wonderful about the turkey Mr. Hearst is going to give us." John answered abruptly, "It sure is. I don't know why he would give us a turkey instead of our regular Christmas checks." Then he walked away. This news traveled faster than the turkey tale. The hilltop was in an uproar. Finally, Norman Rotanzi had to talk to each of his men individually to get this rumor straightened out. Norman told his men, "You cannot believe one thing John Harris says, especially when he whispers." Well, we got our Christmas checks in spite of John's rumors. In 1947, my check was $75.00.

John Harris, the prankster.

The Shah
Of Iran's Visit

I received a note from Ann asking if I would run a show for
the Shah of Iran, who was coming to the Castle on Christmas
Eve.

*Note from Ann Miller asking Byron Hanchett to run a show for
the Shah of Iran.*

The Shah Reza Pahlavi and Empress Soraya, his wife, and their entourage, arrived at the Castle on Christmas Eve. The Shah was driving alone, trying out a new Thunderbird. He was stopped for speeding just north of Santa Barbara, driving eighty miles per hour, but he was not given a ticket.

Ann was organizing dinner for them in the Refectory, when she saw water dripping down from the ceiling. She called Norman Rotanzi and me to investigate. We went upstairs to where the Shah's General had his room. The General did not understand how the mixing valve on the shower worked, and he had accidentally broken the shower valve off the wall and water was squirting everywhere. Norman and I immediately shut the water off, and Ann moved all the place settings down the table, so the General's bath water did not drip in their champagne.

After the excitement was over, we told Randy Hearst what had happened, to which he responded, "Move him to another room. He will just have to general someplace else." We moved the General to another room, and explained to him how the shower worked.

After running the show for the Shah of Iran, Randy Hearst took me down to the wine cellar. He said, "Pick yourself out a bottle of wine for Christmas — take any bottle you want." Not knowing the quality of wine, I chose it the American way, thinking the biggest was best. I picked a magnum of champagne — and it was the best.

When the Shah left, he gave us a very generous tip; mine came to $40. The Shah was the last world-famous person to see a show in the theatre.

Changes In Castle
Operation In 1949

Mr. Hearst left the Castle in 1947 and there were few guests left. In January 1949, the Castle was changed into a smaller, more economical operation.

In the kitchen, we put in an electric stove to replace the large water wheel stove. This electric stove had made the rounds. It started its service at the ranch house, to the airport, and then to the Castle. In 1984, it still has the same plug I put on it in 1946.

Electric water heaters were put in the kitchen, under the kitchen, and in the top of the servants' wing. These heaters replaced a large oil burning boiler.

In the basement near the electric shop, two more electric water heaters were cut into the hot water lines, which replaced another large oil burning boiler that served the upper rooms of the Castle.

We also changed the water heaters under the guest house, so one could be used instead of four.

The three large transformers under the tennis court were disconnected, backfeeding the power from the transformers just outside the kitchen. Everything was put on standby operation.

A high scaffold running to the top of the servants' wing, used to pour concrete, was torn down.

The scaffold used to pour concrete on top of servants' wing; torn down in 1949.

The power and telephone lines going to the construction camp, stables, and carpenter shop were torn down. Lights to the tennis court were disconnected. The power to the boilers to heat the pools was cut.

Sometimes I think I disconnected and tore down more than I installed. I'd hate to have the reputation as being the man who tore the place down.

The State's
Operation In 1958

In 1958, Mr. William Randolph Apperson, the ranch superintendent, called me to do some telephone work at the ranch, which I did. He wrote a note for me to give to Norman Rotanzi at the Castle, in which I was instructed to move all the surplus materials out of the Castle before it was given to the State.

Note from William Randolph Apperson to Norman Rotanzi.

I made two trips hauling old magneto, crank telephones, motors, tools, and surplus materials from the Castle to the ranch before the State took over. I also tested the siren at the ranch. As I drove down the hill with the materials, I knew a part of my life was ending, but I was glad that so many other people would have an opportunity to see the Castle. I wondered if I would ever work at the Castle again.

I did go back and work for the State at the Castle in 1965, under Arliegh Barnhizer (Barney). I spent two years rewiring the Castle and enjoyed my work with the State.

In one room, the ceiling was one complete painting, and a light fixture hung in the center of this painting. The fixture had no electrical box. The State inspector said that if there's going to be a fixture in the ceiling, it must have a box.

I set my ladder up and was ready to cut in the box, but Barney said to me, "Byron, hold off on that until I get permission to cut a hole in the ceiling." Barney checked with Ann Miller and, two letters and three phone calls later, we had permission.

I used a 3-inch hole saw to cut a hole in the center of the painting, just big enough to fit the box. Ann had a picture taken of the ceiling before I cut the hole. Then a picture was taken of the hole, and another picture of the piece that came out of the hole. The piece was then labeled and put in the antique vault. I was amazed at the State's effort to preserve everything as much as possible.

The Theatre Equipment
And
Telephone Office Display

In December of 1982, Ann Miller called me requesting to see some pictures of marble statues I had taken at the Castle in 1946. She wanted to check these pictures against other more recent pictures, which would tell her if there were changes in the marble caused by weather or erosion.

Ann invited me to take a tour of some of the places we worked in 1946, one of which was the theatre projection booth. Ann left me with my thoughts for a moment to take care of another matter. How things had changed.

I looked in the back of the booth, and there was all the old equipment and the two projectors I had run. I was glad to be alone, because when I saw them, the memories came rushing back. Not only memories of the Castle, but I had run projectors like these when I went to junior college, and my wife was a theatre cashier when I married her.

Back then we used to hold theatre parties inviting students and other young people. One type of entertainment was to run film cuts. These film cuts were mistakes stars had made while shooting a picture. Those film cuts are now known as bloopers. Some of the cuts had four letter words in them, often used by the stars, because of these words they could not be run in a theatre for the public. Mothers would warn their daughters to stay away from those terrible theatre parties. The film salesmen would leave these cuts as a friendly gesture to get the theatre managers to book more of their films.

Another type of entertainment was to run two news reels at the same time, using the picture of one reel and the sound of the other reel. One particular combination was of J. Edgar Hoover making a speech, with the sound of another reel describing dogs at a dog show. The sound reel was talking about the square muzzle and the good conformation of this bull dog. Many funny situations were created in this manner. Another comical situation was a fashion show as the picture with a rodeo as the sound.

When we ran Pathe News, it showed a rooster crowing at the end, and at the beginning of an MGM picture it showed a lion roar. A good projectionist could make the lion crow when the lion threw its head back and opened its mouth.

Ann came back to the booth. She looked at the old machines and then at me, "Byron, what can I do with these old machines? I would like to display them on one of the tours, but I have no one to set them up." I started talking, and when I finished talking I had volunteered two months of my time.

Then she took me to the theatre basement and showed me a lowered section of the floor. This basement was to have been a bowling alley and the lowered section was for the pinsetters. She told me the marble now stored there could be moved to another place, making room for the display.

Monday morning, Bill Southerland, Russel Bearce, both state employees, and I went to work. The floor was leveled and rugs put down. We moved all the old equipment from the projection booth, and set it up like it was when in operation. Young Lewis, a projectionist in San Luis Obispo, donated film and a lens that was missing, and the booth display was finished.

While in the process of leveling the floor, we went into a vault to get lumber, and sitting there on the floor was the old PBX telephone switchboard. I found tags that I had put on it in 1947. At one time, eighty phones were connected to it. We also found a dictaphone, dictaphone shaver, and a cabinet for the teletype machine, which had all been in the telephone office and Col. Willicombe's office. I asked Ann what she was going to do with this equipment. She pointed to more marble and said, "We can move this." I knew what that meant.

We moved the PBX telephone switchboard and everything that had been in the old telephone office. We also moved all of the equipment that was once in Col. Willicombe's office, including the shortwave radio and microphone.

After Forrester Warren, a state employee, helped me with some of the mechanics involved, we had a complete display of the telephone office and the theatre booth. It is now shown on Tour #4.

Display of the old theatre projection room and telephone office put together in 1983. On the left is the projection booth, and on the right is the old telephone office.

The PBX board, dictaphone, and shortwave radio that were once in the old telephone office.

Gerald Fialho, State superintendent of the Castle, presenting Byron Hanchett with a plaque for creating the theatre equipment and telephone office display.

Ann Miller and Byron Hanchett after completing the theatre equipment and telephone office display.

Mr. Hearst

Mr. William Randolph Hearst

Mr. Hearst's card.

It's difficult for new people coming to the Cambria and San Simeon area to understand the feelings that old timers and local people have for the Hearst family and the Castle. There is a loyal, protective attitude, as one would have toward an old friend.

This place has been home and job security to many. Many learned an occupation and earned a living in this community due to Mr. Hearst.

Many stories are told about Mr. Hearst moving trees, protecting animals, etc. Some of the stories have been twisted and altered. Some stories make him appear to be eccentric. He was not eccentric. He was sensitive to nature.

An unusual example of his sensitivity to his surroundings is the path behind "C" House going to "A" House. This path, made with beautiful stonework, ran under the limb of an oak tree. The limb was eight inches in diameter and reached across the path about three feet above the walkway. To walk on this path, one had to either climb over the limb or under it. When Mr. Hearst purposely left this limb, he probably said, "This is one tree they will have to look at." His awareness of nature was not out of necessity, but wisdom.

The oak limb across the walkway behind "C" House in 1946.

Byron Hanchett in 1983 on the walkway behind "C" House with the oak limb gone.

In writing my experiences, I am not implying that I had a one-to-one relationship with Mr. Hearst. I never had that opportunity. A person did not need this relationship to know the man. His works spoke for him.

In 1919 he hired a woman, Miss Julia Morgan, as his architect. Many men, even today, let alone back in 1919, would not have hired a woman architect, even with her accomplishments.

Many people pay much attention to Mr. Hearst's wealth. He spent $5 million on construction, $3 million on his art collection, and $1 million on architecture. Yet, in 1951, the Castle was assessed at $56 million. Many love to hear these figures rattled around, but they are only looking at the surface

196

of the man. The interesting thing is not his money, but his attitude toward wealth; he used, shared, and enjoyed it.

Mr. Hearst had many interests and enterprises. He had cattle ranches, radio stations, newspapers, interests in movie productions, art, and architecture, and he ran them all.

One of his greatest assets was the way he eliminated detail. Henry David Thoreau once wrote, "We live menially, like ants. Our life is fretted away by detail." I have two letters in my scrapbook which demonstrate what Mr. Hearst did with detail. If someone wrote a letter to him asking for instructions, he would write his comments in the margin of the letter, or he would just write "okay," and then send the letter back to its originator. This made communication simple and easy. One letter to Marks Eubanks had three paragraphs containing only three sentences.

THE CALIFORNIA OREGON POWER COMPANY
Dunsmuir, California

September 13, 1944.

William W. Murray, President
Sunical Land and Livestock Department
Hearst Magazines, Incorporated
409 Hearst Building
San Francisco 3, California.

*Mr. Hunter —
Please see that
these things are done
WRH.*

Dear Mr. Murray :

In compliance with your recent telephone request, our District Superintendent, Mr. Pearson, accompanied by Mr. Lucero, a lineman, inspected the distribution circuits at Wyntoon on September 12.

Mr. Pearson's report indicated your outside lines are in a good state of repairs. However, he suggests that the following changes be made :

1. The 11 K.V. transformer serving the caretaker's cottage is protected by 5 K.V. fused cut-outs. These cut-outs should *O.K.* be replaced by 11 K.V. cut-outs.

2. The above condition also exists at the transformer serving the buildings at The Bend. *O.K.*

3. Transformers located in the old power house building should be installed outside on a suitable platform or on a pole. These are outside type transformers and the adjoining building is used *O.K.* for sleeping quarters.

4. The only protection to the six transformers installed in the three vaults and serving the new cottages, and the only means of disconnecting these transformers, is located on the junction pole where the 11 K.V. line goes underground. This makes it impossible to disconnect or do any work on any transformer without disconnecting all the transformers and disrupting service to all of the cottages. Individual cut-outs should be installed for each *O.K.* transformer.

In order to make a load check on the various circuits in the building it would have necessitated turning on the various heaters, appliances and lights. Mr. Eubanks did not care to do this. Apparently he was quite reluctant to do anything that might excite Mr. Hearst. *Nonsense! Why does not Mr. Murray refer these people to me. I will tell them how I feel about it.* If we can be of any further assistance to you, please advise us.

Very truly yours,

THE CALIFORNIA OREGON POWER COMPANY
H. M. Edmonds

A letter with Mr. Hearst's writing in the margins, showing his desire for simplicity in communications.

September 27, 1944

Mr. Marks Eubanks,

Wyntoon.

Dear Mr. Eubanks:

You have made a wonderfully clear and com-

prehensive report.

We are all very appreciative of your valuable

assistance.

Let me express my personal thanks.

Sincerely,

W R Hearst

Another letter from Mr. Hearst to Marks Eubanks illustrating the brevity of his communications.

History has shown that many men with influence and power go through life like a bulldozer, pushing and shoving people and things out of their way, making a path for themselves. Other men with great wealth believe this gives them a license to waste. They act like someone trying to sample all the flavors of life, rushing from table to table with their mouth full, trying to taste.

In order for one to properly use power and wealth, there must be culture. Mr. Hearst had more culture than wealth. I know of few men with such power and wealth who have helped so many others to help themselves.

When I look back upon my past experiences and the people from whom I have learned, I think of Mr. Hearst and his Castle. They have been a great stepping stone in my life, and I am grateful for having had that experience.